THE SEVEN KEYS
TO
SUPEREFFICIENCY

THE SEVEN KEYS
TO
SUPEREFFICIENCY

WINSTON FLETCHER

SIDGWICK & JACKSON
LONDON

First published in Great Britain in 1986 by
Sidgwick & Jackson Ltd
Copyright © Winston Fletcher 1986

ISBN 0 283 99340 5

Phototypeset by Falcon Graphic Art Ltd
Wallington, Surrey
Printed in Great Britain by
Biddles Ltd, Guildford, Surrey
for Sidgwick & Jackson Ltd
1 Tavistock Chambers, Bloomsbury Way
London WC1A 2SG

CONTENTS

INTRODUCTION:
THE SEVEN KEYS
TO
SUPEREFFICIENCY

In moments of saintly honesty – or utter desperation –
most of us will admit that we could, and should, be more
efficient than we are. We know that with a little more
thought and care our working lives could be less shambolic, less frustrating, better organized – and much more
fun. We would have more free time to think, to manage, to
maximize our own potential and success.

It isn't necessary, it isn't even possible, for any human
being to be perfectly and unremittingly efficient. But you
have probably read books or been on courses and learned
how to manage your staff, your department, your company. *Superefficiency* will simply tell you how to manage
yourself.

Before embarking on the process of improving your
efficiency it is vital to state what efficiency is (and is not).
Dictionary definitions are not much help. Misconceptions

on the subject abound. Here are some of the most common:

> *Efficiency is a nice neat and tidy desk with everything laid out at right angles and all the papers elegantly stacked*
> *Efficiency is just an obsessive attention to detail*
> *Efficiency is a characteristic of small, pedantic minds: to be wildly disorganized is a sure sign of creativity*
> *Efficiency only matters when you're at the bottom of the ladder; it's unnecessary when you are planning grand strategy at the top*
> *Efficiency is something you should be able to leave to a good secretary*
> *Efficiency is either in your genes or it isn't; if you were born inefficient, give up the struggle – relax and enjoy it.*

None of the above is true and all of them constantly impede our striving for greater efficiency. Here, in contrast, are the facts:

> *Though chronic untidiness almost inevitably results in inefficiency, chronic neatness is no proof of efficiency at all. You probably know lots of neat and tidy people who are chronically inefficient*
> *It is impossible to be efficient if you never pay attention to detail, but attention to detail is a symptom, not a cause*
> *Efficiency liberates, it does not constrict; the majority of highly creative people are also highly organized*
> *Few, if any, reach the top of the ladder without being exceedingly efficient; the higher you climb the more crucial efficiency becomes*
> *Secretaries can be marvellous aids to efficiency but, despite office mythology to the contrary, even the most marvellously competent secretary cannot organize a hopelessly incompetent boss (mainly because marvellously competent secretaries won't work for hopelessly incompetent bosses)*
> *While some people are naturally better organized than others, efficiency is a skill which can easily be learned – a set of methods and techniques with which you can vastly improve your capability and performance.*

Perhaps the overriding misconception about efficiency is that it is principally to do with things – diaries, sharp pencils, filing cabinets and so on. It isn't. It is principally to do with human beings – yourself and those you work with. So we'll embark on the process of achieving super-efficiency by concentrating on the crucial link between one human being and another – the link which seems so often to break and lead to monstrous inefficiencies – *communication*.

Then, in turn, we will examine the other six keys to superefficiency. You will learn how to manage your *time*, defeat *procrastination*, master *data*, generate winning *ideas*, *travel* more creatively and handle *people* more effectively.

With these seven keys you can deftly turn the locks which bar your way to greater achievements, greater success – and *superefficiency*. Read on.

1

HOW TO
COMMUNICATE
PERSUASIVELY

Once upon a time, when bosses were bosses and erring employees could be fired at the drop of a paperclip, people who bungled instructions soon found themselves on the wrong end of a boot. Today the boot has changed feet. In today's ethos, if I misunderstand you it is probably your fault. If I understand you perfectly but do not like what you are saying I will prevaricate, procrastinate and quite possibly thwart your request entirely. So improving your ability to communicate is the first key to improving your efficiency.

Think about it for a moment. You can get nothing of any significance done at work without the help of others. The craftsmen of yore could chisel out their goods alone, but you can't. You can advise, recommend, instruct, make decisions, give orders, but all of those involve other people. Even individuals who work individually – like journalists or barristers – continually rely on others. In our extraordinarily complex economy the prescient words of the great sixteenth-century metaphysical poet John Donne ring truer than ever: 'No man is an island.'

So the more efficiently you can cope with other people

the more efficient you will be. And the secret of coping with people efficiently is *persuasive communication.* Persuasive communication is not salesmanship (although salesmanship is one form of persuasive communication). Persuasive communication is communication presented in the form most suitable to its recipients; in a form, in other words, in which it will persuade them to do what you want them to do without further ado.

Persuasive communication thus saves time, and time-wasting is one of the essences of inefficiency. But persuasive communication provides two subsidiary benefits. First, in modern organizations, particularly large organizations, how you say things is often more important than what you say. Many major companies are living proof of the triumph of style over content. We all know this to be true of appearances: no matter how brilliant your brain or how decisive your decisions, if you wear crumpled clothes and scuffed shoes you'll never get to be chairman. It's the same with communication.

Second subsidiary benefit: in any organization those who are frequently misunderstood soon get known as bumblers. If half the executives in the world were aware of the way their secretaries, subordinates and colleagues mocked and mimicked their waffle they would sharpen their thoughts or become paranoid, or both. It isn't possible to cope efficiently with people if even before you open your mouth they know you're going to bumble.

In a sense everyone knows all this. Nobody deliberately bumbles. So why do so many of us communicate poorly? What are the barriers to better communication? Is it possible, with a modicum of effort, to teach ourselves to communicate persuasively? The answer, simply, is yes: communication is a skill we learn unconsciously while growing up, and any skill we've learned unconsciously we can consciously learn to improve.

Personal Communication

Let's start with personal, face-to-face communications.

Over recent years psychologists have devoted many studies to the problems of personal communication and how to overcome them. Their findings are important and are, happily, broadly consistent with plain common sense. Here are the six principal lessons to be learned:

1. MAKE SURE YOU HAVE YOUR LISTENER'S ATTENTION

Most of us cope with the unending babble in which we live by switching off our ears from time to time. At home we do not always listen with total and undivided attention to our spouses or kids. We learn to recognize subconsciously, from the intonation of their voices, whenever they are saying something to which we ought to listen. (Unfortunately we often get it wrong, which is why 'You're not listening to me' must be the most commonly uttered phrase in every family in the world.)

More unfortunately still, we transfer our bad habits from home to work. We doodle and daydream in meetings; we brood about last week's lost squash match instead of concentrating on last week's lost sales. And as we do to others so they do to us.

Fortunately there are simple ways to cope with the problem:

Speak up, speak up A surprisingly large number of people – we all know some – unwittingly speak so quietly they are especially easy to mishear or even to ignore. It's a practice to which insecure and shy people are particularly prone, and they commonly compound the problem by putting their hands in front of their mouths. All of which, needless to say, irritates listeners and encourages them to switch off. There is no point in talking unless you wish to be heard. If you suspect you speak too quietly ask a friendly colleague, someone you know will tell you the truth. And never speak with your hand in front of your mouth: apart from muffling your voice, it will imply you are not telling the truth (see 'Control your body language', page 6).

Modulate your voice Monotonous speakers turn listeners into sleepers. Actors teach themselves to modulate their voices, and so can you. Once again, ask a close colleague whether it is a problem from which you suffer, or listen to yourself on a tape recorder and use the tape recorder to help you improve.

Enthusiasm and irritation Occasionally raise your voice a few extra decibels to communicate enthusiasm or irritation. Many highly successful business people, particularly in large companies, vociferously employ the power of positive agreement to communicate their determination and drive.

Ask confusion-detector questions Get into the habit of asking a confusion-detector question at the end of any complicated instruction. Not a 'Were you damn well listening to me?' question, but a gentle yet specific query referring to something you've said, like: 'Are you absolutely sure you can deliver the quantity of rubber grommets I mentioned by next Thursday?' One or two such confusion-detectors – they won't take a second – will rapidly establish whether or not your messages have been received, so you can relax and go over and out.

KEY TIP Psychologists have proved people are unlikely to be listening to you if they are looking away from you, so never give instructions to the backs of people's heads.

---

2. DECIDE WHAT YOU'RE GOING TO SAY BEFORE YOU OPEN YOUR MOUTH

Here again many of us transfer our bad habits from home and pub to office and factory. To think before speaking is an effort, and in most aspects of life it is unnecessary. Our natural inclination is to start chatting and optimistically assume that somehow, somewhere along the way, we will communicate what we intended to communicate, if we even knew what that was when we started.

Never begin a sentence unless you know how you are going to finish it. Never feel embarrassed about pausing for a few moments to collect your thoughts before speaking: 'Fools rush in' applies as much to utterances as to actions, whereas 'He's a thoughtful speaker' (and 'thoughtful' equals 'unhurried') is always a compliment.

Most people who waffle entangle themselves in long, convoluted sentences. Don't. Speak in short simple sentences. They will be easier to prepare in your mind. And easier for the listener to understand.

The advantages of thinking before you speak are inestimable, but care must be taken to avoid a couple of undesirable side effects. Having decided what you are going to say, once you start you may talk too quickly and without sufficient explanation; or you may cram in too much and create what psychologists call 'information overload'.

The best safeguards are to watch your listeners' faces – their reactions will tell you whether or not they are keeping up with you – and to finish with a couple of confusion-detector questions.

3. SPEAK THEIR LANGUAGE

As the psychologists put it: messages that are not encoded clearly clearly cannot be decoded. And the code must be the listener's code, not your own. Every business creates its own jargon and – worse still – the burgeoning use of computers is resulting in an ever increasing use of code numbers and acronyms. Every company has products and projects called 664F and MIPS (unless they're called F466 or SPIM). Within the company most people, but not everybody, probably know what 664F and MIPS refer to; to people outside the company they are utter gibberish. Yet I have attended more meetings than I can count at which people chattered on about their 664Fs and MIPS seemingly oblivious of the fact that many of those present had no idea what they were talking about.

So don't use jargon, code numbers and acronyms unless you are *certain* everyone present knows what the hell you are talking about.

4. NEVER FORGET PEOPLE ARE ONLY HUMAN

Many if not most of the things you say at work will provoke some kind of emotional reaction. At the very minimum the reaction may be: 'Oh dear, this means more work'; at the maximum you may provoke fear, anger and resentment on the one hand, or enthusiasm, hope and joy on the other.

Occasionally – as in all human relations – you will say something which seems trivial and mundane to you, but which sparks off a seemingly inexplicable and unwarranted emotional reaction. Life at work is full of such tiny traumas and it is unwise to get too bothered about them, but remember that:

(a) when people are emotionally upset they do not hear or remember accurately what they are being told – this often occurs when people are being fired, and almost always with unfortunate after-effects

(b) if the number of such incidents appears to be increasing this will indicate a deterioration either in your own performance (if it happens with a lot of people) or in that of the particular colleague concerned (if it happens with just one). If the former, you will need to pay close attention to this chapter on improving your powers of communication; if the latter, gently draw the colleague's attention to the problem and – this will need great tact and care – suggest ways in which it could be overcome.

5. CONTROL YOUR BODY LANGUAGE

Non-verbal communication and body language have been faddish subjects in the popular press over recent years. What a pity the more sensational articles are not true. How easy life would be if we could buy little body-language dictionaries which would tell us what everyone else was really feeling and thinking deep down in their subconscious. Sadly, non-verbal communication and body language are not that desperately exciting or dramatic, but that is not to say they are unimportant. To quote Professor Michael Argyle, one of the foremost researchers in the field:

> Human relationships are established, developed and maintained mainly by non-verbal signals, although of course words are also used.... We are only partly aware of non-verbal signals from others, we are hardly ever aware of the signals we are sending ourselves. These non-verbal signals constitute a silent language which, although they may be the more important aspect of an encounter, operate largely outside the focus of constant attention.

Argyle's experiments have led him to conclude that non-verbal signals have about four and a half times the effect of verbal ones; however, a leading Californian researcher, Albert Mehrabian, claims that the facial expressions of a speaker are almost eight times as powerful as the words used.

Whichever figure you choose to believe, there can be no doubt that non-verbal signals play a key role in persuasive communication. On average in conversation we look at each other for about a third of the time. To look less often or to look away determinedly conveys boredom and lack of interest; to stare continuously almost always causes embarrassment; but to look at the other person slightly more often than average conveys enthusiasm and liking – a strong basis for persuasive communication.

Other important body-language rules are:

> Always lean forward in your chair rather than slouching back in it: leaning forward shows interest and enthusiasm (watch the best TV chat-show interviewers)
> Make sure your verbal and non-verbal messages do not

conflict: if you make a hostile statement in a friendly voice, with a smile, the listener will discount the hostility and perceive the message to be friendly. (This was established scientifically by Professor Argyle and four colleagues in 1970.[1])

You can communicate anger or irritation without saying a word, by clenching your fist, gently banging on the table or drumming with your fingers

Don't cover your mouth with your hand: as mentioned above, it betrays uncertainty about what you are saying and suggests you may well be lying. (Our subconscious psyches are often a good deal more honest than we are.)

Keep a wary eye on other people's body language: when people rub their noses it usually indicates that they are puzzled; when they shrug their shoulders they are indifferent; when they hug themselves they are feeling threatened.

Controlling your own body language and watching other people's will at first make you hyperconscious of every tiny movement. That won't last long and quite soon, like all skilled communicators, you will intuitively be using non-verbal signals to help you put across your point of view persuasively.

6. BE A GOOD LISTENER

This chapter began by pointing out how crucial it is to make sure you always have your listener's attention. Now let's reverse the message by stressing that communication is a two-way process.

The most common bad habit is to start thinking about what you are going to say long before the other speaker has finished. This often adds rudeness to inattentiveness, since once you have determined what you intend to say there is a fair chance you will brusquely interrupt the other person in your determination to say it. The old quip, 'Don't talk while I'm interrupting', neatly pinpoints this habit. It's a habit that should be kicked.

Moreover, hearing, as everyone knows, is not listening. Listening is not a passive activity. To train yourself to listen more effectively here are seven brief rules, based upon the researches of American psychologist Robert C. Beck[2]:

Be empathatic Put yourself in the other person's shoes, both intellectually and emotionally.

Be attentive Force yourself to concentrate; don't allow your mind to wander.

Be patient Accept that others may be less good communicators than you are and don't impatiently jump to conclusions.

Don't be too clever Being faced with someone who seems to know it all makes people clam up for fear of looking foolish.

Ask for explanations Never be frightened to ask people to explain points or words you have not fully understood; it is always far better to ask than to get things wrong.

Ask 'opening up' questions 'Opening up' questions are open-ended (like 'Would you tell me more about that?'); they cannot be answered with a mere yes or no and provide no clue as to the answers the questioner might want to hear.

Use self-disclosure Admitting to your own problems and difficulties will encourage others to be open and honest about theirs.

If you can increase the efficiency and effectiveness of your personal, face-to-face persuasive communication, then mastering the arts of written and other forms of communication should be comparatively painless. This is hardly surprising, since personal relationships are basic to our nature and existed long before memos and telexes were ever dreamed of.

Remember that, just as a bad workman blames his tools, a bad executive blames everyone in sight for failing to understand him.

KEY TIP It is always worth apparently wasting a few minutes ensuring you have been understood at the outset to avoid wasting a few days when it transpires that you haven't.

Telephones and Telephoning

Surveys have shown that on average 90 per cent of executives spend over an hour a day and 40 per cent of executives spend two or more hours a day on the telephone, so it's hardly surprising that the telephone is one of the greatest sources of inefficiency in business life.

Telephone inefficiency is of three types:

Making calls inefficiently
Taking calls inefficiently
Managing calls inefficiently.

Let's look at each in turn.

MAKING CALLS INEFFICIENTLY

This is the least important of the three types of telephone inefficiency; it comprises making calls without sufficient preparation, making calls at bad times and failing to get through.

Before making any call which is going to cover more than a single, or at the very most two, topics, write out a list of the points you want to cover and tick them off as you deal with them. If you don't, you can bet your phone bill to British Telecom's share price that as soon as you ring off you'll remember something you've forgotten and have to phone again.

Likewise, before making any call – particularly any international call – think whether you've chosen a suitable time. Phoning just before lunch or just before the company shuts up shop and the switchboard closes down is unlikely to be ideal, unless you deliberately want to ensure the conversation ends quickly (as you frequently will).

Before making international calls always check the time change. If all the wasted international calls made daily throughout the world could be added together, the cost would probably exceed New Zealand's gross national product, and that excludes the cost of the man hours wasted in making them. Even the most experienced international businessmen do it all the time; there's no need for you to emulate them.

Many modern telephones have programmes which automatically put you through to people who were out when you called, as soon as they return and are available. However, failing to get through to people who are permanently 'out' when you call is a challenge and one which, particularly if you are selling, must be overcome. It would be nice to be able to say that honesty is always the best policy and sometimes it is – but often it isn't. So here are three devious tips which frequently work:

1 Ask for people by their first names or nicknames; if questioned as to what your call is about, reply that it's personal. (The now famous chairman of one of Britain's top advertising agencies, when he was younger and less famous, instructed his secretary to bypass the secretaries of important prospective clients by sounding as though she might be the client's mistress. Immediately she got through she switched the call back to her young boss. How this ruse would work with female clients is unclear!)

2 Avoid secretaries who screen calls by phoning before or after hours; busy executives usually come in early and stay late

3 Call the chairman's office first. You will then be referred or transferred to the proper department and calls routed via the chairman have a not altogether surprising propensity to get through.

KEY TIP   Group all your outgoing calls together, set aside the time necessary to make them each day, block it out in your diary, and don't allow yourself to be distracted. Otherwise making calls can be as disruptive as taking calls, and as inefficient.

TAKING CALLS INEFFICIENTLY

The ring or warble of a telephone is well-nigh irresistible. Almost all of us will interrupt almost anything we are doing to lift the receiver and stop the noise. If you work in sales or customer service that is obviously the right thing to do; for others it may not be. Many successful executives have disciplined themselves to break the ringing-phone addiction and continue with their work, secure in the knowledge that if it is important the caller will call again.

Obviously one of the principal roles of a secretary is to intercept calls and let through only those which she knows to be important (see above!). If she is to do this efficiently you must brief her thoroughly. Regularly during the day you must let her know whether or not you are willing to take calls, and if so which calls you are willing to take. An intelligent secretary will use her own judgement as to which calls sound urgent and important, but she can only do so within the guidelines you give her. Moreover, she must at all times deal with callers with tact and diplomacy. Some executives boast of having secretaries like dragons who breathe fire on unwanted callers. Apart from being gratuitously rude, fire-breathing dragons fare ill when the unwanted caller turns out to be the chairman of the company's largest customer.

However, even the most rigorous defence system will

occasionally be penetrated, and you will find yourself talking to somebody you do not particularly want to or, worse still, you particularly do not want to. You then need to close the conversation rapidly but without rudeness. Here are three sentences with which to bring such calls to an abrupt end:

'I'm afraid that doesn't interest me at all, and I'm extremely busy just now so I must ring off.'
'You really shouldn't have got through to me as I'm in a meeting so I must ring off.'
'I was just leaving the office and I'm terribly late so I'm afraid I must ring off.'

They all work perfectly, but doubtless you can invent your own polite put-downs which will better suit your personal style and be equally effective without being offensive.

KEY TIP **Your secretary should never say you are available before she has checked with you. She should invariably say, 'I'm not certain if he's in the office, I'll just see.' Any other course of action inevitably leads to callers feeling slighted, often quite unnecessarily.**

MANAGING CALLS INEFFICIENTLY

There are two ways in which necessary calls can be made inefficiently: (a) if the callers fail to communicate, or (b) if the calls go on too long.

Most of the rules of successful, persuasive communication are the same for telephone conversations as they are for face-to-face conversations, with three additions, all of which arise from the fact that telephone conversations necessarily exclude the non-verbal body language of communication:

Avoid instant judgements A surprisingly large number of people mistrust and dislike using the telephone; as a result their telephone manner is often stilted and inept. Do not automatically assume that because the person at the other end sounds hesitant or gauche they are unenthusiastic or hostile.

'Smile' while you talk   This will help overcome any nervousness at the other end and will make you sound friendly, persuasive and confident.

Speak dynamically   Avoid long pauses which will make *you* sound diffident and unenthusiastic; if the conversation goes on and on, stand up and gesture as if the other person were in the room with you. It will be reflected in your voice.

And talking of conversations which ramble on and on, we come to the second kind of inefficient call management. Even if you have carefully prepared your list of topics and decided precisely what you are going to say, there is a fair chance that the other person will take his or her time and prattle on interminably: telephones frequently have that effect on people. (It is doubtless another consequence of the lack of non-verbal communication – they cannot see how bored you are.)

Have you noticed, for example, that when people call long distance the first thing they usually ask about is the weather? Invariably you give them a weather report and then ask for theirs in exchange. Since neither of you is about to visit the other, what difference does it make what the weather is? Sometimes such apparently pointless conversations are intended to ease the way into the serious purpose of the call. If so, fine, but they hardly need go on as long as they do ('Is it really raining that hard . . .?').

If you're striving for superefficiency you will bring most telephone conversations to an end as quickly as possible. If, however, you are having serious trouble bringing down the curtain then:

(a) claim that your secretary has just told you there's an

urgent long-distance call from Tokyo waiting to get through

(b) knock loudly on your desk and say you have to hang up as someone is at the door

(c) tell the caller the connection has got so bad you can no longer hear what he or she is saying, then hang up in the middle of one of your own sentences; nobody ever imagines you would hang up on yourself.

Alternatively, if you know the person to be a telephone windbag, call during the lunch hour or when you know he or she will be out and leave your message with someone else.

In addition to the above rules of telephone efficiency here are some guidelines which will help you control Alexander Graham Bell's wonderful invention instead of allowing it to control you:

Get up-to-date equipment   If your organization has not installed the most up-to-date equipment available, bring as much pressure as you can on it to do so, and lobby your colleagues to do likewise. Modern instruments, with pre-coded dialling, transferred calls and automatic call-backs make living with the telephone infinitely more bearable.

Note callback numbers correctly   Always ask, and get your secretary always to ask, strangers to repeat their number twice if you need to call them back. The number of times that I have called back wrong or nonexistent numbers is too embarrassing to remember.

Keep a record   Always jot down immediately anything of any significance said to you over the phone. For most people telephone conversations are even harder to remember than face-to-face conversations and there is a strong likelihood that details not committed to paper will be forgotten.

Watch out for drinkers Remember it is quite possible (particularly if you call immediately after lunch) that the person at the other end may have been drinking. If he or she were with you in the room you could probably see the effects, but on the telephone you can't. This is a more frequent, and more serious, problem than most people realize. If you are at all suspicious, then:

(a) without giving offence, try to ascertain the truth – asking jokey questions can often help
(b) note down especially carefully anything important that is said by either side. Topers are just as likely to forget what they've heard as what they've said.

Keep a telephone log If your job requires you to use the phone a lot, consider keeping a log. It should have the following simple headings along the top of the page:

Date
Time
Name
Number
Topics to cover/Topics covered
Action required.

With such a log always to hand it is almost impossible to use your telephone inefficiently. On the contrary, compared to the great majority of telephonic fumblers you will, once again, achieve superefficiency.

Telex

Those who work for British companies rarely realize the extent to which telex machines permeate the lives of executives working for multinationals. Many senior executives working for American companies talk despairingly about 'management by telex', because each and every day telex messages start flooding in shortly after 2 p.m., when their American head office opens (it's 9 a.m.

over there). The telexes then continue throughout the afternoon, often demanding instant answers, almost as intrusively as telephone calls.

If you work for such a company you will long ago have learned that it is essential to do work calling for continuous concentration in the mornings. If you are contemplating taking a job with such a company it is wise to ascertain in advance whether 'management by telex' is the company style. If it is, you will have to decide whether or not you can live with it.

Used correctly, telex machines are a great aid to efficiency, almost as instant as the telephone, with the advantage of providing a written record. However they should not be used, though by bullying managers they frequently are, as a substitute for the telephone when unpleasant messages need to be delivered. Executives who lack the mettle to communicate disagreeable news face to face or on the telephone often hide behind the telex. They use it to transmit messages they would never dare utter in person. Don't do it: it is poor communication and so it is inefficient. The telex is a lousy way to communicate feelings, emotions and subtleties.

Those are the don'ts about using a telex. Here are the dos:

Use the telex to confirm immediately any phone conversation during which a mass of data has been discussed

Use the telex to confirm immediately any phone conversation which may have legal consequences

Use the telex to ask for complicated information

Use the telex to provide advance warning of future data requests, travel arrangements, etc.

Use the telex when the other office is closed due to a time change or local holiday (particularly if your own may be closed when they re-open).

Above all, remember that although the telex is virtually instantaneous it is not a telephone; and although it uses paper it is not a letter. Most telex messages are transmitted by telex operators and this makes them unsuitable for confidential information. The medium influences the message, and telexes look, and feel, brusque and public.

Putting It in Writing

Since writing is a skill learned at school, which most of us have been practising for donkey's years, it is astonishing how insecure most of us are about our writing ability. Indeed, it is astonishing that so many intelligent, well-educated executives write so badly.

It is astonishing because, while it is undoubtedly difficult to write like a Wodehouse or a Waugh, it is quite easy to learn how to write clear and effective business documents. Dazzling verbal artistry is not required: you merely need to master and adhere to four basic rules, some of which have already been alluded to at the start of this chapter.

THINK BEFORE YOU WRITE

Before writing anything down always think out carefully the totality of what you want to say. Not just the first few sentences or paragraphs, but the entire message. Many business reports, letters and memos are confused and confusing because their authors attempted to think them out as they wrote. If writing helps you to think and to clarify your thoughts – which it almost always does – then it is essential to use your first effort as a rough draft and to revise it with gusto, root and branch.

KEY TIP   You'll save a lot of time and effort if, instead of writing out a complete draft, you jot down the principal points you wish to communicate, in logical sequence, before you start.

WHO ARE YOU WRITING FOR?

Are you addressing one person or several? Are they completely ignorant of the subject and in need of background information? Do they expect or require the document to be laid out in a particular way? How do you want them to react (see 'Anticipate reactions', page 20)? If you are calling for action, is it absolutely clear who should do what and by when? If some people are getting the document simply 'for information', have you made that obvious? If people's superior management will be receiving copies, have you said anything which will cause problems? (If so, make sure you have done it consciously and deliberately: every day, in every organization in the world, a myriad bitter rows break out when one executive's document accidentally throws another executive in the quagmire and – surprise, as the phrase goes, surprise – the quagmired executive refuses to believe it was an accident.) So while you're carefully thinking out what you're going to say, think equally carefully about who you're saying it to.

NOBODY WANTS TO READ YOUR DOCUMENT

Unlike novels and magazines, it is normally a safe bet that nobody reads business documents for fun. Few things blight the average executive's life more than a seven-page letter or a hefty report landing with a thump in the in-tray. Indeed, only a minority bother to wade diligently through the documents they receive, as the following table shows[3]:

How managers read reports

Summary	100% of the time
Introduction	68% of the time
Body	22% of the time
Conclusions	55% of the time
Appendix	15% of the time

So keep your documents short. Don't wander. Get quickly

to each point. Don't try to be clever or funny: if you could write cleverly or amusingly you would probably be earning your living writing for *Punch*. Keep clearly in mind at all times the objective(s) of the communication. Don't be stuffy or pompous. Don't repeat yourself. And never be too lazy to rewrite something you know, in your heart, you could improve.

George Orwell, author of *Nineteen Eighty-Four* and *Animal Farm*; wrote exceptionally fine unpretentious prose, and here are four of his personal stylistic principles (from *Politics and the English Language*, 1946), which are of particular relevance to business documents:

> Never use a long word where a short one will do
> If it is possible to cut out a word, always cut it out
> Never use a foreign phrase, a scientific word or jargon
>   if you can think of an everyday English equivalent
> Never use the passive where you can use the active.

Correct grammar, proper punctuation and accurate spelling are, naturally, essential to any form of written communication. But it is not the role of *Superefficiency* to help you pass an O-level English examination. If you write in short, clear sentences and follow George Orwell's principles you are unlikely to entwine yourself in complex grammatical misconstructions.

ANTICIPATE REACTIONS

One type of inadvertently provoked reaction has already been noted ('Who are you writing for?', page 19), but every document that makes positive statements can provoke a welter of varying repercussions. An astute author will aim to identify these in advance. 'I never imagined you'd take it that way', one of the commonest phrases heard around most offices, is not so much an apology as an admission of ineptitude.

The quickest way to assess likely reactions to a communication – and remember that when your missive is received you will not be present to explain 'Exactly what I meant by that was . . .' — is to ask yourself three pairs of questions, and apply them to each of the recipients individually:

Will they believe what I'm saying?
If not, how will they challenge it?

Will they agree with what I'm saying?
If not, how will they oppose it?

Will they fear what I'm saying?
If so, what will be the effect on them personally?

If you can predict the answers to these three pairs of questions with a reasonable degree of certainty then it is safe to send your document winging on its way.

Finally, take advantage of the fact that in every job a fair number of letters and queries repeat themselves regularly. Spend a little time drafting standard replies which your secretary, or the word-processing department, can use as you indicate. However, it is vital to draft and deploy such all-purpose letters carefully: few things are more infuriating, more pointless or reflect less well on their sender, than stereotyped answers which are not in fact answers to the questions the questioner asked.

Dictation

A recent American study showed that four out of ten American executives still draft letters by hand, although dictating to a secretary or a machine would improve their output by up to 400 per cent. On the other hand, an observant reader can usually spot when a letter has been dictated because dictated documents are usually less concise and less lucid than their handwritten counterparts.

To ensure that any lengthy documents you dictate are both lucid and concise it is vital to:

1 Jot down an outline of what you intend to say before

    you start (as with written documents, but even more essential)

2 Tell your secretary (or dictate into the machine) roughly what the document is about, again before you start, so that she can follow the thread

3 Pause for a few moments before each sentence, to get what you want to say absolutely clear in your mind before it comes tumbling out of your mouth

4 Discipline yourself to speak more succinctly and less repetitiously than you probably do in normal conversation.

Never be afraid to ask your secretary whether your dictation makes sense and is utterly clear, or if she can think of the right word when your mind has gone blank. Your aura of power and wisdom should not diminish in her eyes; if it does she's a lousy secretary and you'd better find another.

Whether dictating to a secretary or to a machine you should speak slowly but not funereally. Emphasize consonants that can easily be misheard, like 'b', 'p' and 'd'. Spell out proper names and difficult words. State in advance whether or not you will be providing punctuation.

If you have any doubts whatsoever as to whether you have dictated the document perfectly, ask for it to be bashed out quickly and roughly, in double spacing with lots of room for corrections. The rule that applies to written documents applies with still greater force to dictated ones: never be too lazy to amend a document you know in your heart you could improve.

Your reward, if you follow these few simple rules, will be that your dictated documents are as articulate and precise as your written ones – even the keenest observers won't be able to tell them apart – and you will be able to increase your 'written' output superefficiently.

Meetings

It has been estimated that some 50 million meetings are

held throughout the world each day, and in no area of business life are the six rules of persuasive communication more crucial. Every large organization is stuffed full of committees and meetings, many of which are prodigious timewasters and grossly inefficient. As Dean Thomas L. Martin of the Southern Methodist University in Dallas put it: 'Of all possible committee reactions to any given agenda item, that one will occur which will liberate the greatest amount of hot air!'

In order to manage and manipulate meetings superefficiently it is first necessary to clear away some widely held misconceptions as to their purposes and functions.

Most people optimistically believe meetings are called to make decisions. Rarely. Social psychologist A. A. Harrison has listed the five purposes of meetings as follows[4]:

The pooling of skills and resources
The division of labour
Group members can stimulate each other
Members may be made more considerate of others' problems
Members can encourage and support each other.

Harrison then added four disadvantages with which regular meeting-goers will doubtless be all too familiar:

There are frequently conflicts among members
Social norms and conformity destroy novel ideas
People are reluctant to speak because they fear negative evaluations from others
People in groups either argue or have fun: either way they devote less time to the task in hand than do individuals working separately.

Or, as leading management guru Harvard Professor Peter F. Drucker – admittedly slightly overstating the case – wrote in his classic work *The Effective Executive*[5]: 'One either meets or one works. One cannot do both at the same time.'

With such cautions in mind, let us consider how to make the best of meetings.

Define your objectives Before going to a meeting, decide what *you* want to get out of it. Research shows that the average meeting comprises eight people, all of whom are there for their own reasons: make sure you know what yours are.

Deal beforehand with the practical matters Read the agenda and background papers, if any. Obtain additional information – preferably information unknown to anyone else – on any points upon which you intend to make a contribution. Ensure that you are ready for any solos you may wish to perform. Check the time and venue of the event. (There are no frequent meeting-goers in the world who have not, on occasion, found themselves in the wrong place at the right time or the right place at the wrong time.)

Analyse the other participants Difficult though this sometimes is, it is idle to attend any meeting without having made strenuous efforts to discover who else will be present. Once you know, it is worthwhile making further strenuous efforts to discover their views and prejudices on those subjects in which you yourself have an interest.

Learn to manipulate meetings To be a truly effective meeting manipulator you must master the seven deadly skills of meeting behaviour. These are, in alphabetical order:

AGGRESSION Everyone admires, though few like, people who are aggressive in meetings. Studies show aggression in meetings to be surprisingly uncommon. Well under 1 per cent of all statements 'show antagonism'. That is why, adroitly used, it is so effective. Tone of voice and subtle use of body language normally suffice: when you look and sound furious people believe that you are furious.

CONCILIATION The great psychologist Konrad Lorenz has

shown that aggressive animals can be pacified by appeasement signals and submissive postures. Likewise in meetings, aggressors can be both defused and confused by overtly conciliatory behaviour. But don't be unctuous. On the contrary, the more forceful you are most of the time, the more surprising and effective your occasional apologies and admissions of error will be.

ENTHUSIASM   Whereas aggression and conciliation should be used sparingly, enthusiasm is something of which you can hardly have too much. Anyone with the resilience to stay perky through the unending flow of interminable convocations which most of us attend will frequently – and deservedly – be able to put one over on the other participants when they are comatose or even asleep.

INTERROGATION   Used cunningly, questions can delay decisions ('Hadn't we better wait till we get all the facts . . .?'), can incite arguments ('Are you seriously trying to claim that . . .?') and, above all, can be used as camouflaged statements which could not possibly be made in a positive form ('I don't suppose there's any chance that one of your team is getting a kickback on this deal, is there?' or 'Wasn't it Davidson-Clarke who was caught with his secretary in the stationery cupboard?'). The well-honed question can be lethal.

PATIENCE   Contrary to popular belief, few successful people are impatient, though they may often employ impatience as a form of simulated aggression. In meetings patience allows you to listen to the arguments advanced by the other combatants, perceive who is on whose side, prepare your own case, pick your moment, and win.

SULKS   The use of sulks must be rationed vigorously. Their sole aim is to elicit sympathy, and if you sulk too often you quickly become known as a Moaning Minnie and ignored. However, properly deployed sulking can help you win worthwhile victories by exploiting worthless defeats – you sulkily sacrifice a point that is trivial to you in order to gain sufficient sympathy to win a subsequent argument you care about.

WITHDRAWAL You hardly need a doctorate in business studies to know that you can, mathematically, withdraw only once per meeting; and, sensibly, only once every few months at the most. It is a high-risk action since, if the meeting goes against you after you have left, you've had it. None the less, properly timed and stage-managed withdrawals – as politicians and trade unionists well know – can precipitate complete chaos and confusion (successfully allowing those who have run away to live and fight another day – which, of course, was their objective).

By deploying the above skills you will find you can get meetings and committees to reach the right conclusions – the ones you want them to – astonishingly often. So, from your point of view at least, they will no longer be so grossly inefficient or such prodigious wastes of time.

KEY TIP If you enter a meeting without any personal objective you will most certainly exit without any personal achievement.

Presentations

Statistics on the subject are unavailable, but almost all executives find themselves called upon to make presentations from time to time. On such occasions they are very much in the spotlight, so executives who handle them well do themselves a power of good. (Naturally the converse is also true.)

The overriding golden rule about presentations – and speeches (see below) – consists of just one word: rehearse. Whether out of indolence, conceit or embarrassment, many executives try to get by without rehearsing presentations. Usually it ends up as a massive bungle. Even if they do manage to get by, that's the best they do; with rehearsal they could certainly have done better. That is not a hint or a tip; it is an inviolable commandment. If Brando, Guinness and Streep need to rehearse, so do you.

But even before you rehearse you must get your presentation right, and here are the rules for preparing successful presentations.

Prepare your visual aids Keep your visual aids simple: always use the minimum number of words and/or figures possible; make sure they will be legible to everyone in the room; make them look professional but not expensive; make sure they are in the right order and the right way up. (Kodak's Law states unequivocally that any slides that can be upside down will be upside down.)

If you are presenting away from home, always arrive early and check the equipment, the room and the seating arrangements.

Prepare yourself Dress your best so that you can intrepidly take centre stage and be glared at. Speak confidently; uncertainty can be charming and winning, but not (or very rarely) in presentations. Stand rather than sit. Without becoming stilted or awkward, try to control your non-verbals – your expressions, your gestures, your poise. Don't stare at your visual aids: address the group.

Prepare the presentation The following important findings come from psychologist W. J. McGuire's major study 'The Nature of Attitudes and Attitude Change'[6]:

1 Open by explaining briefly what you are going to say and why
2 Create the expectation that you are going to solve the audience's problems and/or satisfy the audience's needs
3 Put the positive case in terms that are relevant to the audience
4 Raise and reject the obvious objections
5 Be continuously responsive to the audience, watch

their reactions. Explain points that appear to have been misunderstood

6 Speak loudly and distinctly, but never sound superior
7 Control your anxiety or it will disrupt your message
8 Accept comments (and even criticisms) seriously and sympathetically or you will lose the support of even your supporters
9 Avoid confrontations
10 At the end draw the conclusions explicitly, especially conclusions for action.

In many organizations presentations are now becoming an art form in their own right, with ever higher standards constantly expected, so before finishing let's repeat once more and without apology: rehearse, rehearse, rehearse.

KEY TIP If you draft your visual aids on small pieces of paper – I always tear A4 sheets in half – it stops you crowding them with too much data and forces you to keep them simple.

Speeches

Almost all the rules that apply to presentations apply equally to making speeches (particularly the one about rehearsal!). However, speeches are different from presentations in two key respects: there are no visual aids for the audience to watch, so all their concentration will be upon you; and because most of the speeches that people hear are made by semi-professionals – politicians, actors and the like – their standards of comparison are painfully high. So the first thing to say about making speeches is that if you fear you are not good at it, avoid it. Outside politics, many people get to the top without ever making a speech.

However, effective speech-making is palpably another

useful weapon in the persuasive communicator's armoury, and if you have a natural talent it is well worth developing. As with most other human activities, the more you practise the better you'll become. To help you get started here are some useful pointers:

Decide the main messages you want to get across; don't clutter your speech with irrelevant details

Establish the size and composition of the audience in advance

Almost nobody – not even the greatest orators – can speak brilliantly off the cuff, so either speak from clearly legible notes or from a written text; notes are best

If using notes, write down the first few lines to get started, and the last few lines to help you finish positively and strongly. Speeches that peter out with a whimper are embarrassing (and counter-productive)

Use your own handwriting or a jumbo typeface – ordinary typewriter print will be too small to read easily. Consider using different colours for greater legibility

Again, if using notes, try writing them on cards – ordinary postcards – and number the cards clearly in case they get out of order

On each card put a few key points – single words or brief phrases – to act as prompts and reminders

Write timings on the cards so you can keep to your schedule. Make sure you can see a clock or put your watch where it is easily visible, otherwise you are bound to go too quickly or take too long and irritate the audience

Whether using notes or a text, look out at the audience *at least* 80 per cent of the time

Don't stare fixedly ahead, but look around at everyone, encompassing them all in your interest. Don't bob up and down or wave your arms about or put your hands in your pockets

Think carefully of the sensitivities of your audience: for

example, avoid blue jokes if there are women present. Even if the women don't mind, some of the men
will be embarrassed, and embarrassment is conta-
gious
Unless you are *sure* you are a witty speaker, don't try to
be a stand-up comic and above all don't use funny
voices. Audiences will be sympathetic to one
(perhaps less than hilarious) opening joke, and one
closing joke – but for most speakers, that's their
ration.

KEY TIP Never worry about being hideously nervous
before a speech – almost all the best speakers are, and
it's probably nature's way of preparing you to perform
at your peak. Some people suggest neck exercises and
deep breathing immediately before your performance
will aid relaxation, and in so far as they are a distraction
they may provide some solace, but nothing really
obliterates nervousness. Whatever you do, don't try to
drink your nervousness away: that road leads to inco-
herent ruin.

Salesmanship

At the start of this chapter it was pointed out that
persuasive communication is not simply salesmanship;
but salesmanship is the touchstone of persuasive communication, and most of the rules and tips above comprise the essence of successful sales technique. Nor is
Superefficiency intended to be a textbook for salesmen,
but there are few, if any, executives who will not find
themselves selling something to somebody at some time.
Indeed, it is doubtful whether anyone utterly lacking the
wiles of salesmanship could ever be an effective executive.

Super-salesman Harry Turner, in his excellent book *The
Gentle Art of Salesmanship*[7], divides all successful sales-

people into two types, tigers and foxes. Before trying to improve your own selling skills you should decide which type you are:

Tigers	*Foxes*
Physically strong	Softly spoken
Highly articulate	Physically unimpressive, but smartly dressed
Fashion conscious	
Weak on detail	Thoughtful, even scheming
Weak on planning	
Gregarious	Brilliant at detail
A shade flashy	Strong on planning
Theatrical (good platform speaker)	Retentive memory for minutiae
A fondness for food and drink	Most effective in one-to-one situations
Keen on sport and exercise (to counterbalance the above)	Quietly fanatical about succeeding
	Bookish, music-loving

The importance of this categorization is twofold. It shows that there is no single formula for sales success; and it implies, correctly, that if you are one type of salesperson you needn't and shouldn't try to be the other.

Indeed, while cynics accuse selling of being one of the most meretricious of human activities, the truth is that Shakespeare's great maxim, 'To thine own self be true', applies in selling at least as forcefully as it does elsewhere. As Harry Turner states:

Clients can sniff out a phoney very quickly. Even dumb clients. So be yourself. Embellish by all means. Trim, polish, duck, weave, react to special circumstances by a touch of fine timing, *but stay true to your basic character.*

Numerous academic psychological studies have confirmed Turner's learned-at-the-sharp-end advice. However, to embellish your natural talents, here are five simple principles which would help you to sell ice cream to the Eskimos:

Get people to say yes   As Professor H.A. Overstreet writes in *Influencing Human Behaviour*[8]:

> A 'no' response is the most difficult to overcome. When a person has said 'no' all his pride of personality demands that he remains consistent with himself. He may later feel that the 'no' was ill-advised; nevertheless there is his precious pride to consider! Hence it is of the very greatest importance that we start a person in the affirmative direction.

Don't try to win arguments   When you're selling you can't win an argument: if you lose you lose, and if you win you lose.

Don't shun sweet talk   Everyone knows flattery won't get you everywhere, but it can help you sell an awful lot.

Or sweet listening   We've already noted that good listening helps communication; it is also highly flattering. Inexperienced salespeople think selling is all about talking and having the gift of the gab; experienced salespeople know it's almost the opposite.

Smile   This has become such a dog-eared maxim that you may feel insulted at its mention, but any advice on selling which does not stress the importance of smiling is culpably negligent. Every bit of psychological research on the subject shows you're more likely to put across a case convincingly if you do it with a smile.

KEY TIP   Dale Carnegie said: 'Remember that a man's name is to him the sweetest and most important sound in the English language.' Successful salespeople never forget it.

You should now be a master of persuasive communication. So it is time to address the second key to super-efficiency – the art of time management.

2

TIME MANAGEMENT

Keeping a Time Log

Some years ago Ivy Lee, often called the father of management consultancy, gave the following advice to Charles Schwab, the then president of the mighty American Bethlehem Street Corporation:

> Number the items you have to do tomorrow in the order of their real importance. First thing tomorrow morning, start working on number one and stay with it until it is completed. Next take number two and don't go any further until it is completed. Then proceed to number three and so on. If you can't complete everything on schedule don't worry. At least you will have taken care of the most important things without getting distracted by items of lesser importance.

Lee asked Schwab to test the system and to pay him whatever it was worth. Within a few weeks Schwab posted a cheque for $25,000, a vast sum at the time, worth at least ten times as much today.

Lee's advice – prioritize your tasks, then deal with them one by one – is the basis of all modern time management. However, to the average executive in the average large company it sounds like a wonderful, utopian dream, out of touch with reality by many million light years.

A few company presidents may be able to lock their doors, guarded by secretaries and PAs, and methodically work through their work in the cavernous silence of their thickly carpeted offices. But out in the frenetic hubbub of everyday executive life an endless welter of interruptions and demands – many of them emanating from the aforementioned president himself or his equivalent, and therefore not to be ignored – gatecrash each day's schedule, shattering the cool calm of contemplative toil. (I must add that in my experience exactly the same applies to most company presidents, but maybe Schwab was an exception.)

Perfection being unattainable is no excuse for throwing in the towel. Chaos and confusion need not reign supreme. The fact that for most of us most of our days are disorderly and disorganized means that there is vast room for improvement: even quite small reforms can yield worthwhile rewards.

How, then, can you set about managing your time more systematically? The first and most crucial step is to divide your time, as rigorously as you know how, between *private* time and *public* time: between those hours which you devote to the company of others (either personally or on the telephone) and those which you devote to working alone.

How can you calculate the correct division? Tedious though it may sound, the only way – and happily there will be numerous subsidiary benefits, as we shall see – is to keep a time log for a few weeks (four at the very least).

Nobody enjoys keeping time logs. At first just keeping the time log itself seems to absorb an inordinate amount of time. Yet within a few days it will seem to take no time at all. After a couple of weeks it can become addictive. You may start to feel a compulsive need to record your timekeeping obsessively.

Nevertheless, it is rarely worthwhile keeping a time log permanently – and it's an easy addiction to break! The profound insights into the way you spend your working day which a time log will provide can generally be gleaned in a few weeks; after that it is only worth starting

to use one again – and it is then *well* worth starting again
– when the nature of your job changes.

A basic time log is just like a daily diary with three
columns:

Time started/Ended	Activity	Hours/Minutes spent

At the end of each day you add up the total amount of
time spent in each of the following activities (it doesn't
take long), watching out for patterns of good time usage
and time wastage:

	Hours/Minutes	% of day
In meetings (groups):		
In meetings (one to one):		
On telephone:		
Handling interruptions:		
Thinking/Planning:		
Writing/Dictating – letters:		
– documents:		
Dealing with short-term crises:		
Other_____:		
Other_____:		
Other_____:		

In addition to the three columns given above, many
people find it useful to add a fourth. This column, usually
placed on the extreme right, will contain your own
estimate of how well you think your time was spent –
from a maximum of 100 per cent if you think the activity
was exceedingly useful and productive down to 0 per cent
if it was a sheer waste of time.

Some people find such mathematical assessments a
little too arbitrary and difficult to make; certainly it is
unproductive and a waste of time to sweat too long over
whether a particular activity was 23 per cent or 24 per cent
unproductive or a complete waste of time. None the less,

if you can keep a fourth column, even roughly, it will provide you with more precise knowledge of when and where your time is wasted and when and where it isn't.

Once you have kept your time log for a few weeks you must spend a few hours with your calculator, assessing how much time you need, on average:

For private work – thinking, writing, planning
For meetings
For telephoning
For emergencies.

You will then know why, in the past, you have so often found yourself unable to cope with a last-minute demand for an urgent report or have built up a huge list of return phone calls which lingered on your desk for days. Almost certainly you have not been balancing your job's time demands satisfactorily, with super*inefficient* results.

More importantly still, the use of a time log will provide strong guidelines for the prioritization of your activities. The setting of priorities, and their achievement, will be covered fully in Chapter 3, but it should already be apparent to you that accurate knowledge of how your time is spent is essential to ensuring that you devote more time to tasks of great importance and less to those that hardly matter. Which is probably precisely the opposite of the way you are spending your time at the moment!

KEY TIP Don't cheat: the time log is for your personal use. If you've spent time gossiping or reading an old copy of *Cosmo* or phoning friends, log it. Only when you know the truth can you decide whether or not to change your habits.

Mastering Interruptions

Reducing unwanted interruptions is a crucial aspect of

any time-management programme. Obviously an intelligent secretary, if suitably positioned outside your door, is the best possible way to keep unwanted interruptions at bay, and if you are fortunate enough to be thus endowed many of the rules below can be delegated to her. Nor are all interruptions necessarily unwanted: a surprise telephone call from a customer intending to make a large purchase is rarely unwelcome (even if you yourself do not work in sales or marketing).

Nor is it wise to shut yourself away all day and become the Howard Hughes of the organization. Do so, and you will rapidly find yourself out of touch with what is happening, as people stop bringing their difficulties and ideas to you for discussion and help. You'll only hear about problems when they become crises.

(Many modern companies – those in the mammoth Mars/Pedigree Petfoods Group, for example – employ open-plan offices for everyone, up to and including the chief executive, to stop such unsociable behaviour; despite this, however, determined lone wolves manage to create invisible buffer zones around their desks which other people find virtually impregnable.)

The best solution is to let everyone, including your boss, know when you are involved in *private* work and cannot, barring real emergencies, be disturbed. (Incidentally, if bosses have any sense at all, and if they know you're serious, they will try to avoid interrupting you; they know the problems and should realize that it is hardly in their best interest to sabotage your work.)

Such demands for seclusion are more likely to be accepted, and respected, if your colleagues know that you are generally on call. However, even when your door is metaphorically wide open it is vital to establish guidelines that will minimize the timewasters that have been spotlit by your time log.

Apart from the telephone, which we dealt with in the last chapter, the most common interruption is the drop-in visitor. Some drop-in visitations are necessary, some are unnecessary, others simply run on too long. Here are ways to deal with both the latter:

Set time limits   As soon as the visitor arrives and you've learned the reason for the visit, simply say, 'Do you mind if we wrap this up in ten minutes as I've an awful lot on at the moment?' After this it should certainly be possible to wrap the thing up in a quarter of an hour.

Consolidate visitors   As with telephone calls, block out a period of time every couple of days (your time log will indicate roughly how long you need) and ask drop-in visitors to come back. This system offers the added advantage that it is easy to curtail discussions without rudeness when it is apparent that another visitor is waiting impatiently to see you.

Transfer the call   As soon as you know the reason for the visit, say politely but firmly, 'I'm sure X could deal with this better than me. Why don't you go and see him?' It is astonishing – until you keep a time log – how much time most of us spend discussing problems we aren't empowered to resolve.

Invent a meeting   If you neglected to set a time limit and the discussion drifts on endlessly, suddenly look at your watch and rush off to an 'almost forgotten' meeting. Even if you merely go to the loo and return after five minutes, the likelihood is that you will have saved time, but be ready with a follow-up excuse in case you accidentally bump into the visitor you have just ditched!

Order a memo   Almost as soon as the visitor has started speaking, interrupt and say, 'Look I'm sorry but I haven't got time to consider the point properly just now – so could you drop me a brief memo about it instead?'

Visit the visitor   If you know the visitor is a waffler, don't let him start but offer to go to his office a little later; it's always much easier to leave than to lever someone out.

There are three types of interruption which, if they recur frequently, are symptomatic of serious inefficiencies:

Follow-ups When the visitor begins: 'Where is the whatsit you promised by Friday?' the problem isn't the visit, but poor communication or poor organization, or both. If you knew the whatsit was going to be late you should have issued an advance warning; and if your whatsits are frequently late you are probably suffering from the ravages of procrastination, which you will learn how to cure in the next chapter.

Staff queries When subordinates continually seek clarification of due dates, decisions, advice or information you can be fairly certain that you have been failing to communicate effectively, in which case a revision course in the six rules of personal communication is urgently needed (Chapter 1).

Crises, crises If almost every interruption heralds an emergency, something is grievously amiss; the problems may stem from you, or from somewhere else in the organization. First, check carefully that you yourself are not the gremlin and then, if you are utterly certain you are in the clear, cautiously draw the matter to the attention of your boss so that a more widespread investigation can be initiated.

Probably the most common cause of continual interruptions is having too many interactive relationships, be they with subordinates, colleagues or bosses. So yet one more benefit you can derive from your time log is to use it to tot up how many people within the organization you get involved with in an average week. The probable answer is: too many.

KEY TIP Identify all your working relationships, see whether any can be cut immediately, and aim definitely to shorten the list by at least 10 per cent over the next six months. (Make a note in your diary to check you've done it.)

Larks and Owls

American psychologists have established that about one in four people is more efficient in the mornings, the larks; similarly one in four people functions best in the evening, the owls; the rest show no strong leaning in either direction.

Larks open up the office, owls get castigated for being late; larks leave work exhausted by six o'clock when the owls are just getting into their stride. If there's an important job to be done urgently, larks get up early while owls stay up late.

A lark's body temperature rises rapidly after awakening, stays at a plateau and begins to fall at about seven in the evening. An owl's temperature rises gradually throughout the day and doesn't start to drop until 8.30 or later. A body temperature rise is associated with a rise in alertness and a dip in temperature with diminished alertness.

By the time we reach our twenties most of us have a fair idea whether we are larks or owls or neither. If you are uncertain, it is important to complete the following Sleepiness/Alertness table for three consecutive average workdays. It is based upon the famous Californian Stanford University's Sleepiness Scale:

	a.m.			*p.m.*				
	6-8	8-10	10-12	12-2	2-4	4-6	6-8	8-10
1 Alert, wide awake energetic	1	1	1	1	1	1	1	1
2 At a high level but not at peak	2	2	2	2	2	2	2	2
3 Awake but not fully alert	3	3	3	3	3	3	3	3
4 A little foggy, relaxed, let down	4	4	4	4	4	4	4	4

In the middle of each two-hour period put a circle around the number that most closely reflects how you feel. After three days it should be clear whether you are circling most 1s and 2s in the morning and most 3s and 4s in the afternoon (you are a lark) or vice versa (an owl), or whether the distribution is fairly random (you are neither).

For superefficiency you must, of course, reserve your personal metabolic prime time for your most complex and creative tasks, carrying out more mechanical and humdrum jobs during less alert periods. In addition, it is important, if a trifle depressing, to note that Benjamin Franklin's clean-living aphorism, 'Early to bed, early to rise, makes a man healthy, wealthy and wise', has been confirmed, in part at least, by a study of American medical students in which the goody-goodies who went to bed early and got up early generally got better grades.

Diaries

For most of us keeping a diary is one of our earliest imitations of executive life. We fill in our name, address, birthday and the first day of term. Then we lose it. We almost certainly received the diary from our dad, who received it from a printer, one of many he received from suppliers, none of which he wanted because he always bought his own.

The ubiquity of diaries as presents is, in a way, a tribute to their indispensable role in business life. And having kept a diary, more or less, since the age of six, most of us never bother to think about using them more efficiently than we do; familiarity has bred perhaps not contempt, but casual thoughtlessness.

Frequently this results in our losing our temper with our diaries when things go awry (bad workmen and their tools, as ever). Instead of which, by following a few sensible rules, we could vastly improve the efficiency of our diary-keeping. Here they are:

Always use a pencil Executives' appointments get shuffled about with unfailing regularity, and diaries completed in ink or ball-pen quickly become a scratchy, scrawly, illegible mess. Use a pencil, rub out, and insist your secretary does the same.

Use a 'changeability scale'   To help your secretary, and even yourself, know which appointments can easily be changed and which cannot, mark them with asterisks, from zero to three. Zero-asterisked appointments can be moved with ease, those with three asterisks can only be changed in the event of war and/or bloody revolution.

Decode your scribbles   Diary entries are usually scribbled in quickly and illegibly when you are on the phone or in meetings. Rub them out and rewrite them so that you yourself can read them (you'll never decipher them in ten weeks' time) and others can read them as and when necessary.

Estimate endings   All diary entries show when appointments begin, but few detail when they are likely to end, although this information is equally vital to you, your secretary and anyone else trying to fit appointments around those already there.

Doubling up safely   If you keep both a pocket diary and an office diary, and as a busy executive it is all but impossible not to, ensure that you correlate them every day or every other day at the worst; that you mention to your secretary appointments you've made while out of the office whenever you phone in; and that you prohibit your secretary, or anyone else, from making immovable appointments while you are away, since as sure as God made daft little diary pencils, you yourself will be making an equally immovable appointment at that very same moment, in your pocket diary, wherever you happen to be.

Above all, remember that business diaries are not, as so many executives seem to think, top-secret documents. If you want to keep a secret diary full of clandestine little notes to yourself, that's your affair (indeed, that may well be the reason); but business diaries exist to help you and others schedule your work efficiently. This is emphasized in up-to-the-minute hi-tech companies where diaries are computerized and all the executives can call up each others' schedules on their VDUs.

Appointments

We have already discussed the best ways to deal with unscheduled visitations, but all executives commit themselves to scheduled appointments which also prove to be pointless. Often they have a fair premonition of this at the time they make the appointment; on other occasions it becomes painfully apparent within moments of the appointment starting.

Many of the methods for dealing with such appointments are similar to those for dealing with unscheduled visitors:

Set a time limit, a very short one, once you've perceived the meeting to be purposeless

Transfer the visitor, ideally to an amenable subordinate whose time is less expensive than your own. (N.B. Don't use this trick with bad-tempered subordinates unless you *want* the visitor to be treated discourteously.)

Invent a meeting: 'I'm afraid the chairman has summoned me to a vital meeting in nine minutes so I really can't spend long with you.' (N.B. Odd time lengths are always especially believable.)

Ask for it in writing, on the grounds that you had not previously realized how important/complex/detailed the subject has turned out to be.

One type of appointment which regularly demands to be foreclosed more rapidly than seems polite is the disastrous job interview. This applies particularly to secretaries, but can apply to any interviewee at any management level: the moment you meet them you know the chemistry is wrong (and there's a fair chance they feel precisely the same). However, they have already been vetted in three previous interviews and have travelled many miles to meet you. (I have interviewed people for very senior positions who have flown over from California just for the event, and I've then decided within minutes that the wisest thing they could do was dash back to Heathrow forthwith and catch the plane on its return flight.)

Maybe more ruthless interviewers tell the truth bluntly and curtail the appointment immediately. The alternative is to achieve a compromise – to waste as little time as possible without being utterly callous. With secretaries this is comparatively easy, but with senior executives it can be quite difficult – and there are no easy formulas to recommend. However, the guiding principle is to uncover quickly some defect in the interviewees' abilities and to imply that the ability they lack is – whatever they may have been told in previous interviews – in your opinion absolutely crucial for the job.

Here, for example, is an easy one to use with most secretarial interviewees: 'It's almost entirely figure typing, you know. Are you good at typing endless pages of figures? I've been told that some secretaries find it rather boring. They did mention that, didn't they?' This can be guaranteed to get 99 out of 100 applicants scurrying hurriedly from your office, determined to avoid the job at all costs.

Appointments with would-be suppliers are often similar to those with would-be employees: you know they will be fruitless as soon as they start. There is no point whatsoever in dallying unnecessarily with suppliers: it wastes both their time and yours. So let them know quickly and civilly that the appointment has proved to be a mistake; allow them to try to dissuade you for three minutes at the most and then, if they fail, stand up and forcefully conclude the meeting.

Another error we almost all make is to agree to appointments we would prefer to avoid when they are a long way off in the future. It is a convoluted form of procrastination: if you were asked to do it tomorrow you would say no, but you agree to do it in six months' time because that's far too far ahead to worry about. The future then arrives all too quickly, and you either try to cry off at the last minute or go through with the event grudgingly and irascibly.

KEY TIP   Don't accept unacceptable commitments just because they won't happen for ages.

A perfect application of this rule came in a letter I received from a senior Unilever executive whom I had invited to address a conference due to take place over a year later. It ran:

> Your invitation, by giving me so much notice, precludes me from using the usual white lie about already having an engagement on the proposed day of the conference. So I had better tell the truth. I have no thoughts at all on the subject to which your conference is addressing itself, nor is it a subject that particularly interests me. So I would hardly be a suitable speaker. I do hope you agree.

I did.

Finally on the subject of appointments, there is one type of appointment few of us mark in our diaries sufficiently frequently: appointments with ourselves. References have already been made to the need for blocking out diary time for telephone calls and visitors. It is equally, if not more, important to block out *private* time, both regularly (a couple of half days a week or whatever your time log indicates) and specifically, when you need time to work on a particular project. Only by marking such 'appointments' clearly in your diary do you have a faint hope of keeping them free for yourself.

George Bogle, when he was a director of the massive

Reed International paper group, added a useful gloss to this system. One day each month he worked at home, with his secretary, insulated from visitors, meetings and telephone calls except of the most genuinely urgent kind. Throughout each month he collected a file of items to be dealt with on his 'home days'; he swore, believably, that they were the twelve most productive days of the year.

Eating, Drinking and Entertaining

Eating, drinking and entertaining are, at first sight, archenemies of time management and superefficiency. It hardly needs this book to remind us all of the innumerable man hours spent each year by executives guzzling, gossiping and imbibing for two to three hours every lunchtime, or of the deleterious effect this has on their postprandial productivity.

However, it would be naïvely ostrichlike to pretend that the average executive can completely shun the occasional midday beano or, indeed, that the average executive would want to. Moreover, there is no doubt that some kinds of business transaction can be handled better over a meal than over an office desk. Eating together has, since primitive times, been a symbol of friendship, and even today few people find it easy to take a meal with those they dislike. Nor is it a particularly commercial phenomenon: communist commissars and Catholic priests, politicians and academics, civil servants and kings all nosh away, formally and informally, in gestures of brotherly love and goodwill.

So since communal gorging is unavoidable it is essential to do it as sensibly as possible. Here are the rules to help you minimize the damage and maximize the gain:

'There's no such thing as a free lunch' Economics Professor Milton Friedman's famous aphorism is even truer of lunches than it is of economics. If people buy you lunch they will want something in return. It may just be your wildly witty company, but on the other hand . . .

Never accept a meal from someone you've never met
Blind dates may work for teenagers but in business they
result, more often than not, in excruciating embarrassment.

***Don't accept meals from suppliers you know you'll never
use*** It is, to use another teenage analogy, just teasing; as
such, it is likely to end in anguish.

Don't interview job applicants over a meal This once
common practice appears to be on the wane, and rightly
so; it implies too much commitment by the employer and
is difficult to truncate.

Consider carefully how much to spend This is one of
the most difficult decisions associated with entertaining.
If you spend too lavishly you can cause embarrassment or
(if your guests are customers) easily persuade them you
are making too much profit; if you are too stingy you will
equally easily provoke resentment. (Experienced though I
am at business entertaining, I still make both mistakes
from time to time, and then curse myself for having not
considered the matter sufficiently carefully in the first
place.)

Avoid aperitifs and post-lunch libations If you stick to
wine or beer with your meal, and that's all, you may feel
mildly woozy for a little while but you'll be *compos mentis*
for the rest of the afternoon.

Don't compete with champion tipplers Brief the waiter
beforehand to bring you neat tomato juice (or whatever)
when you order a Bloody Mary, and sip your wine by the
millilitre while the tippler gulps his down. As long as his
glass is being regularly refuelled he'll never notice yours.

***Don't aim to make customers happy by making them
drunk*** Let them quaff as much as they want, but don't
press them to take more; the odds are evens they'll dislike
it and blame you, rather than like it and love you.

Don't assume they'll buy anything after a few noggins
Many people get more critical and certainly more aggressive after they've had a few, and can be more difficult to sell to than ever.

Take some exercise to dispel the after-effects Try to squeeze in a brisk, even if brief, walk after a heavy lunch: it will aid your weight, your digestion and your brain.

Having listed the risks and pitfalls, it is now worth briefly reminding ourselves of the benefits to be gained from successful entertaining. Above all, a working lunch allows both sides to glean more about the others' businesses than they possibly could in more formal meetings; each will pick up subtleties and innuendoes, prejudices and trivia, company politics and family problems – knowledge and insights which can make the wheels of future collaboration run more smoothly and more efficiently.

Moreover, while purists (and economists) prefer to believe that all purchase decisions derive from the interaction between quality and price, the reality is that we all prefer to buy goods and services from people we like – whether the people are called Ford or Sainsbury or Mr Kipling or Whitbread. If we entertain successfully then we indubitably enhance our chances of selling our wares.

Of course, not all lunchtime eating and drinking is entertaining (in either sense of the word!). The company canteen, a trip to the pub, a snack in the office – none of these should greatly affect your efficiency, so long as your consumption is moderate. However, not eating at all most certainly will. Recent American research has shown that skipping meals is a rapidly burgeoning American executive habit. People do it because they believe it helps keep them slim and fit, and it allows them to balance their abstinence with a few dry martinis and a gourmet dinner in the evening.

Medical evidence suggests that irregular meal-skipping is unhealthy, which is inefficient in itself. But, more importantly from our particular point of view, it is directly inefficient because it will slow up your thought processes and responses in the afternoon, as nourishment and blood-sugar levels fall. It simply is not possible to attain a high and continuous pitch of productivity throughout the day without sufficient sustenance.

Moreover, as is now well known, the sustenance should be balanced and healthy, high in fibre and low in fat, full of vitamins and with little sugar or salt. There are nowadays dozens of diet books available in any good bookshop. Suffice it to say that it is not possible to achieve superefficiency if you forever feel unwell and are endlessly (and unnecessarily) prey to minor ailments which a healthier diet might prevent. Quite apart from the misery and discomfort it causes you, it's a terrible waste of time.

Before leaving the subject of eating and drinking, a few words about business breakfasts and dinners. Many British executives deride business breakfasts as an uncivilized American habit. That's foolish. Unless you are an incurable owl, who simply cannot open your eyes and mind early in the morning, business breakfasts are an excellent way of adding an hour or so, reasonably painlessly, to the working day. Moreover, because breakfast-times are usually limited and alcohol free, while they are not as sociable as lunches they tend to be more businesslike. They imply urgency and decisions get taken efficiently before everyone scampers off to work.

Business dinners, on the other hand, are the very opposite. They usually can, and frequently do, stretch interminably into the night, and alcohol is often generously imbibed, so that they tend to be occasions more suitable for socializing than for concentrated work. Few executives – except the most owlish of owls – feel competent to solve intricate problems or to have inspired creative thoughts after an exhausting day slaving over a hot desk. (If the evening goes on long enough they may well, in the early hours, become convinced that their inspiration and creativity have returned in full flood; the following morning is unlikely to prove this hypothesis to have been correct.)

So use breakfasts for decisions, dinners for fun, but whatever happens don't – as we shall see in the section after next – try to burn the candle at both ends.

Natural Breaks

Even the busiest executives, at every level of management, occasionally find themselves with time on their
hands. A visitor phones to say he'll be twenty minutes
late, or a document is taking ten minutes to type, or some
essential data won't be ready for a quarter of an hour. As
well as being good opportunities to snatch a few moments' welcome relaxation, these unscheduled natural
breaks can be used for brief jobs which otherwise get put
aside. Some executives find it useful to keep a 'five-
minute job list' of such tiny tasks, which will include
items like:

Prepare meeting attendance list
Draft meeting agenda
Fix restaurant booking(s)
Skim through journals
Make appointments
Personal filing
Arrange tickets for theatre or concert.

Above all, particularly if the natural break has been
caused by a delayed important visitor, use the time to
ensure that you have everything absolutely ready for the
meeting. In the normal course of events, as we rush from
job to job and from appointment to appointment, we
occasionally find ourselves without the right papers or
discover too late a serious typing error in an important
document.

KEY TIP If the fates generously provide you with a
natural break use it, before doing anything else, to
check that all your preparations for the following event
are watertight and flawless.

All Work and No Play

Leo Burnett, the founder of the world-famous advertising agency which bears his name, once sent out a memo to his staff which read something like this:

Dear John Smith,
   I hope you won't object to my sending a copy of my reply to your query to all the agency's staff, but the question you raised is one I know many people in advertising raise from time to time.
   There are, working in advertising, people who fail to realize that advertising is just a job, like any other. They come in early and leave late. They work weekends. They wake up at night worrying about their clients' problems. They rarely see their wives or kids. Like as not, they end up divorced. They have no conversation but advertising. If you meet them at a party they will bore you to tears. They are, in truth, obsessed and blinkered people.
   On the other hand there are, in advertising, many people who realize advertising is just a job, like any other. Except when there are dire crises they arrive around nine o'clock and leave around six. At weekends they play golf, at nights they sleep soundly. They see plenty of their wives and kids and bring up happy, well-adjusted families. They have a wide range of interests, know about politics and the arts, and if you meet them at a party they are a delight to talk to. They are, in truth, well-balanced and civilized people. I just hope we don't have any of them working in this agency.

It was a fine memo, and the myth of the obsessional, blinkered businessman who can spare no time for outside interests is still widely held. Yet it is arrant nonsense. All the greatest and most successful business people have had passionate interests in other fields – horse racing perhaps, or art or music or sport. Even J. Paul Getty, often cited as the archetypal narrow-minded and philistine businessman, was profoundly interested in art (as well as in women!) and founded one of the world's great museums.

It is far from essential to be married to the organization in order to succeed. The very opposite. Scientific research into executive stress invariably shows that it results, in large measure, from too tight a focus on the business and too little, or inadequate, relaxation.

Many executives find sport an ideal relaxant, which provides the additional benefit of helping them keep fit. Others grow addicted to hobbies – from gardening to aeromodelling, from philately to carpentry. Others take up painting or pottery, amateur theatricals or bridge. Winston Churchill built brick walls.

One of the world's leading heart surgeons, now in his fifties, whose work schedule is astonishingly strenuous even by the standards of top businessmen, told me that he plays tennis at least twice a week, not because he hopes one day to win Wimbledon, or even particularly to keep fit, but because 'Hitting a ball very, very hard is the best stress relaxant I know.' Quite how, for other people, the same can be true of lepidoptery is far from clear, yet strangely enough it seems to be.

All that is important is that you should, you must, care about something other than, and in addition to, your work; something more fascinating than dozing off in front of the telly every evening and visiting the pub every Sunday lunchtime for a strenuous game of darts. Modern psychology has, as so often happens, confirmed the wisdom of an old maxim – 'All work and no play makes Jack a dull boy' – but it has gone much farther. All work and no play will make Jack prone to stress, ulcers, impair his decision-making, harm his personal relationships and bedevil his judgement.

Sorry, Leo Burnett, you were wrong. The superefficient executive must find time in his busy schedule for outside interests; otherwise he will soon cease to be superefficient.

Making More Time

The well-worn image, much beloved by television sit-coms and *New Yorker* cartoonists, of father reading the newspaper at breakfast while his exasperated family try to attract his attention encapsulates a basic truth of modern life: there are never enough hours in the day, we never have sufficient time to do everything we want, and the only solution is to do two things at once – even if it means infuriating our nearest and dearest and getting marmalade on our cuffs.

So far this chapter has prescribed the ways to use our normal working hours more efficiently. But are there ways to squeeze a few extra hours into the week without entirely appropriating the very necessary time set aside for relaxation and leisure? Much the best source of extra time is travel, as we'll be seeing in Chapter 6. However, here are three other occasions when you can snatch extra time by doing two things at once:

BATHTIME   Reading on the loo, like reading at breakfast, is a well-worn cliché, but if you are someone who likes to wallow in a tub it is well worth teaching yourself to read documents while you're wallowing. Since writing is impossible a useful tip is to keep a mini dictating machine to hand to note thoughts and ideas for future occasions. (Not a lot of help, admittedly, if you prefer to take a shower!)

ENTERTAINMENT   Yet another well-worn cliché – the business deal that's clinched on the golf course – is likewise a symbol of twentieth-century man trying to have his cake and eat it. However, it is always worth ferreting out the leisure interests of your colleagues and customers since, if they accord with your own, you can sporadically talk business while doing something you enjoy, although it is vital not to talk business incessantly or the enjoyment will soon cease.

HOLIDAYS   Many people believe that on holiday you should turn your back on work and switch off completely – and if that is your view, so be it. However, an alternative tenet states that a change is as good as a rest, and that you can garner extra value (and maybe even extra pleasure) from your vacations by turning them into mini personal academic courses, during which you read some of the many important and stimulating books on business and management which you simply cannot find time to read – and most certainly not in a relaxed and absorbing frame of mind – during the rest of the hectic year. (On the other hand, as with entertainment, under no circumstances should you ruin your holiday by forcing yourself to read Lee Iacocca if you'd sooner be reading Len Deighton; it is, of course, possible to read both.)

Finally, on the subject of time, here is a way to help you manage it without peering repeatedly at your wrist, which is both rude and intensely irritating for other people:

KEY TIP   If you want to know the time look at someone else's watch.

3

STOP PROCRASTINATING!

Knowing how to manage your time is the first step towards defeating that superenemy of superefficiency, procrastination. Now we can administer the *coup de grâce* by learning how to prioritize and how to face up to difficult decisions. Superefficiency cannot make decisions for you, but it will show you how to unlock the barriers which constantly impede your decisiveness.

How to Prioritize

Remember Ivy Lee's recommendation to Bethlehem Steel president Charles Schwab? Utopian though it sounded, it is none the less the basis for all prioritization – analysis. First itemize the jobs you need to do; then rank them in order of importance; then work through them in that order. Is it as simple as that? Not quite. The theory is fine but, as we have seen, it must be tempered by reality.

Quite apart from the problems of interruptions and prior commitments – no sooner have you settled down to a task than someone arrives with an appointment to see you – it is rarely possible to work straight through a job without stopping to get information or plans or recommendations from others. That means delay and, with due respect to Ivy Lee, you can hardly sit around twiddling your thumbs until the point is resolved.

Instead, you start on your next job, which as likely as not will likewise reach some temporary hitch which will need to be resolved before the job can be finished. Hence you find yourself, as always, working simultaneously on four or five (or, more likely, fourteen or fifteen) projects, all of which are urgent, all of which are important and none of which can be completed until you obtain the missing pieces for the jigsaws. (Is it any surprise that executives are so subject to stress?)

Here, then, is a more realistic approach to prioritization. First essential: compile and keep a running 'master list'. Whether on a pad or in a notebook record *every* project, task, assignment, phone call, errand or idea – small or large, trivial or crucial – as it arises. Include all those 'someday I'd like to' activities for which you never seem to have the time (like writing an article for your trade magazine or going on a computer course or whatever).

Since the master list is not intended to be a daily action list there are no restrictions on the number or types of entries. Use it as a catch-all reminder, for everything from getting a birthday card for your secretary to the brilliant marketing idea that came to you in the middle of the night. Beyond highlighting the occasional high-risk tasks (see below) don't bother about categorizing or assigning priorities. The master list is just a sophisticated *aide-memoire*. If you have access to a personal computer, use it – it is ideal for the purpose; if you travel a lot, carry a wallet pad or dictating machine from which you can transcribe items to your master list as soon as you return to base.

A typical master list might read:

Check invoices have been sent to Pumpernickel's
Call Joe re lunch
Speak to Lois about filing
Reschedule date for Pimpernel presentation
Speak to Greg re completely revising copy

Fix meeting with Barry to discuss poor performance
Plan drive to get new clients
Postpone drinks with Freddie
Draft seasonal trends memo.

Tick items once you've started work on them, cross them out when they are finished. Don't waste time rewriting the list every day, but do ensure that old items don't get lost by bringing forward those that are unfinished whenever you turn over a page.

The compilation and continuous use of a master list goes a long way towards forcing you to overcome procrastination. Simply seeing the jobs you haven't yet tackled stare back at you from the list, day after day, will frequently be sufficient to goad you into action. However, to employ your master list superefficiently you should use it as the foundation for a daily 'To Do' list.

Each morning (or evening) run quickly through the master list and:

1   Break down major projects into their constituent parts, putting on the day's To Do list any actions that should be put in hand before the project can be started. This simple form of critical-path analysis will help you avoid incessant delays, of the type mentioned above, once you really start work on a project

2   See if any of the jobs can be delegated to others

3   See whether any of the jobs are, on second thoughts, not worth bothering with and can safely be eliminated

4   Transfer a reasonable number to your day's To Do list, having regard to approximately how important they are, how long they will take, and what else is already in your diary for the day.

It is now important to return to Ivy Lee's advice and rank the items on your daily To Do list in order of priority. The best way is to rank the items as three star, two star or one star according to these criteria:

THREE STAR   Any immediate or critical 'must dos', which you know cannot be delayed for twenty-four hours. Any major project which you have scheduled yourself to carry out that day. Any particularly unpleasant or stressful task, such as criticizing or even dismissing a subordinate for sloppy work.

TWO STAR   Middle-level tasks which need to be completed quite soon, but not necessarily that day. Meetings necessary to progress, or obtain information for, major projects in hand. Jobs that are essential but neither urgent nor unpleasant, such as briefing and report reading.

ONE STAR   Low priority and routine tasks, like responding to unimportant letters and telephone calls, reviewing standard contracts, reading trade journals, completing your expenses.

Avoid trying to use a ten-star or even five-star ranking system or you will find yourself wasting time trying to categorize tasks too precisely: three-star rankings are sufficiently accurate, flexible and easy to use.

When transferring items from the master list, no more than four three-star items, at the very maximum, should go on to your daily To Do list, with the remainder a mixture of two- and one-stars. If you try to pack each day with too many three-stars you will soon abandon the system in frustration: it is not possible to muster the time or mental energy to accomplish more than a few top priority projects each day.

Naturally, as per Ivy Lee's recommendation, you should start the day with the important three-star jobs, so that you can polish them off before turning to the twos and ones. Again as per Ivy Lee, complete each task – or at least reach a natural stopping point – before moving on to the next.

However, don't allow your To Do list to become a fixed and unalterable specification for each day's work. It isn't, and it can't be. It is a route map not a rule book. If you finish your list a little early it doesn't necessarily mean you have worked wonderfully hard and deserve a well-earned rest; more probably it means you scheduled your-self too light a workload to begin with. If, on the other hand, you occasionally fail to complete your list before closing time, you must certainly finish the three-stars, but carry twos and ones over to the next day. That, after all, was the purpose of ranking them in the first place.

KEY TIP   Don't cram every day with scheduled activi-ties: build in a crisis cushion and expect the unex-pected.

Rewards and Risks

One of the cardinal criteria involved in setting priorities has not yet been mentioned: the assessment of the re-wards and risks likely to result from the various activities on your lists.

Almost certainly your working life conforms to the 80/20 principle. This states that approximately 20 per cent of what you do yields 80 per cent of the results and, conversely, 80 per cent of what you do yields 20 per cent of the results. This principle, first propounded by the Italian economist Vilfredo Pareto, operates in many areas of our working (and indeed private) lives:

    20 per cent of customers almost always yield 80 per cent
        of sales
    20 per cent of time spent in meetings generates 80 per
        cent of the results
    20 per cent of a newspaper has 80 per cent of the news
    20 per cent of transactions normally produce 80 per cent
        of profits
    20 per cent of all paperwork yields 80 per cent of the
        value.

And, crucially, 20 per cent of the items on your master list will also yield 80 per cent of your productivity. How can you identify this valuable 20 per cent? (Note that these 20 per cent items are not necessarily the same as the three-star items. An urgent memo from the chairman demanding an instant response may have three stars, yet may in every other respect be a complete waste of time; such illogicalities, as we all know, are among the banes of business life.)

If you analyse your master list and your daily To Do list in the light of the 80/20 principle, you will soon, with a little forethought, come to be able to identify which activities are likely to yield the greater rewards and which the lesser. Obviously the division will depend on your particular circumstances, targets and job, but here are some guidelines which will prove useful:

Cost your time Think of your time as a financial investment ('Time is money', as the old maxim goes) and acquire the habit of evaluating tasks in terms of payoff. Don't devote three hours to making an extra £5 profit on an invoice and then find yourself rushed into deciding on a £50,000 promotional campaign in three minutes.

Identify the high-payoff tasks High-payoff tasks are those that promise to yield substantial or dramatic benefits, like developing untapped markets, devising a winning sales campaign, landing a major contract or substantially increasing productivity.

Minimize the low-payoff tasks Low-payoff tasks are the majority, the 80 per cent of our activities which are neither very satisfying nor very enjoyable but must be done. They are easy to spot on any master list. Try to minimize the time you spend on them; the 80/20 principle isn't immutable.

Finally, there are some tasks which involve *negative* payoffs – or high risks – if they are postponed too long, and you must keep an especially wary eye out for these on your master list. Negative-payoff jobs usually cause domino-like chain reactions when they are delayed. They are often the jobs that need to be done to initiate projects with long lead times, and so they appear not to be nearly as urgent as they are. Normally you are aware of this when you first enter such jobs on your master list and they are fresh in your mind, but the details get forgotten after a couple of days in the hurly-burly.

Bungling such high-risk negative-payoff activities can prove disastrous. That is why you should highlight them as soon as you put them on your master list. It is a sad but unavoidable fact of life that neglecting to undertake positive high-payoff projects will probably pass unnoticed, but neglecting to deal with negative-payoff projects will probably get you fired.

Decisions, Decisions

Every day you make thousands of decisions, most of them unconsciously, with hardly a thought: you decide which clothes to wear, what to eat for breakfast, which bits of the newspaper to read and which to ignore, whether or not to do any exercises, if so which and for how long, and so on throughout the day. Some of these – like cleaning your teeth and slamming the door as you leave – long ago passed so deep into your subconscious that they are now better described as habits than as decisions (although they are habits that you can easily *decide* to break, as, for example, if you are in such a rush you decide there isn't time to attend to your teeth, much as you know you should).

It is paradoxical that we are all, when compared with other species, infinitely decisive, yet most of us feel guiltily indecisive at work. We know we often procrastinate because we are unable to decide with confidence which of the available courses of action is the right one and which the wrong.

So the first vital step is to decide how decisive you really are. To do this Peter Turla and Kathleen Hawkins of the National Management Institute, Texas, have devised the following self-assessment questionnaire[9]:

	Often	Sometimes	Rarely	Never
Score:	(1)	(2)	(3)	(4)

1 Do you have second thoughts after making decisions?

2 Do the opinions of others unduly influence your decisions?

3 Do you procrastinate on making decisions?

4 Do you agonize over making difficult decisions?

5 Do you get bogged down considering so many details it's hard for you to decide?

6 Do you put a dollar's worth of energy into making 1-cent decisions?

7 Have you missed opportunities because you waited too long to decide?

8 Do you let others decide for you on choices that are really yours to make?

9 Did you hesitate as you answered these questions?

Your total score	Assessment
32-36	You are highly decisive, have established your long-term goals, take responsibility for your choices in life and are probably working pretty much the way you like to.
20-31	You find making decisions uncomfortable, but by no means

impossible. You are too susceptible to changing your mind, but you could easily improve your decisiveness with a little guidance and effort.

Below 19   You need to be a lot more decisive. You try to avoid decisions, hoping that they'll go away or that somebody else will make them for you. Because you are not naturally decisive you need to tackle the problem consciously and force yourself to be more resolute.

Whatever your result, unless you scored a full 36 out of 36 your general performance would be improved if you could improve your decision-making. And patently this is not a matter of minor importance. As phenomenally successful Chrysler boss Lee Iacocca states in his autobiography[10]:

> If I had to sum up in one word the qualities that make a good manager, I'd say it all comes down to decisiveness. You can use the fanciest computers in the world and you can gather all the charts and numbers, but in the end you have to bring all your information together, set up a timetable, and *act*.

But how can you decide what action to take? First you must analyse the problem and obtain all the relevant data: this process is described fully in Chapter 5, but for the moment we'll assume you've taken these initial steps – as Lee Iacocca said, they are not going to make your decision for you.

Harvard Professor Peter Drucker points the point somewhat differently[5]: 'A decision is a judgement. It is a choice between alternatives. It is at best a choice between almost right and probably wrong.' Your aim must be to ensure that you are 'almost right' more often than not.

Far and away the best aid to making major decisions was devised by Benjamin Franklin over two hundred years ago. I use it all the time and it never fails. You analyse the decision into 'pros' and 'cons' and write down the two lists facing each other on a single sheet of foolscap. (You must boil down the pros and cons to a few words each, and no decision analysis should ever run to more than a single page, if that.) A pros-and-cons analysis for, say, whether or not to change your job, might look like this:

Pros	Cons
More money	Not a significant increase, not worth moving for alone
More responsibility	
Like new boss	
Success won't be easily achieved: big challenge	Clearly trusted in present job
Nearer home: less daily travelling	Like all present colleagues
More international involvement	New company has not been doing too well, may be foundering
Pleasant working environment	A lot of time spent away from home
Becoming stale in present job	Will no longer have a personal secretary
No promotional opportunities at present available	Present management know I'm getting itchy feet, and will probably find something for me soon
	A bit early to change jobs again

Having carried out the above analysis, my personal decision would be against taking the new job, but yours might be the opposite. Some decisions will always depend on your individual aims and objectives. Ben Franklin's system doesn't turn human beings into automatons, lacking free will; it is an aid to judgement which will help you to be almost right, almost always.

Incidentally, it is vital to put the pros and cons down on paper: don't try to carry them in your head. Only by writing them down can you ensure you are not being slipshod and have identified all the factors. More important still, be honest. There is no point in prejudicing the outcome by biasing the lists. If you know what you want to do, don't waste your own time producing a bogus analysis to justify your decision to yourself. (But it is often well worthwhile producing an honest and realistic pros-and-cons analysis to confirm, for your own peace of mind, that the decision you have already reached is the correct one.)

The pros-and-cons list is the best aid to decision-making yet invented, but life is too short and time is too fleeting – especially at work – for you to write out an analysis before every small decision. Here then are some hints for helping you make run-of-the-mill decisions more effectively:

Pre-determine your objectives   Are you anxious to make a fast buck or more interested in the long haul? Are you keen to be popular or don't you give a stuff? Are you willing to let your home life and work life interact or determined to keep them separate? The more guidelines you can lay down for yourself, the quicker and easier it will be to decide which activities will help you meet your objectives and which won't.

Evaluate the downside   A few years back the word 'downside' was much used in business jargon, particularly in the financial world: the 'downside' is simply the worst that can happen if everything goes awry. The word is no longer much heard, but the concept is still an excellent aid to decision-making: analyse the consequences of your decision coming utterly unstuck – they will rarely prove to be quite as disastrous as you first feared.

Ask the world's greatest authority   More accurately, ask yourself 'What would the world's greatest authority (or your immediate boss, or the company chairman) do in these circumstances?' It will help you approach the problem more objectively by forcing you to see it from a different viewpoint.

Deliberately delay Consciously put off the decision for fifteen minutes or twenty-four hours, depending on the relevant time scale; you will find that it keeps resurfacing in your mind until the right answer emerges.

Seek guidance Have others faced similar problems before? If so, are there any reference books or trade magazine articles which will illuminate the subject and suggest the answer? My first boss taught me that the propensity of executives to reinvent the wheel is prodigious. Surprisingly often you'll find the solution to your problem already exists if you make the effort to search for it.

Help! Similarly, don't be too proud to ask for advice. It doesn't make you look stupid, it makes you look smart, whereas you will indubitably look like an idiot if you make the wrong decision when your colleagues, or your boss, knew the right one all along.

Spin a coin Finally, when all other remedies have failed, try spinning a coin: it is a powerful way of concentrating the mind. If it produces the answer you want you'll accept it, but if it produces the answer you don't want you'll overrule it. After all, people in your position would never dream of letting a coin make their decisions for them, would they?

Now you've decided. How can you stop yourself from changing your mind again, or at least fretting incessantly about whether you've reached the right decision? The wisest advice on this subject was given by the great philosopher Bertrand Russell in his classic work *The Pursuit of Happiness*. First, he urged, think as deeply about the decision as you know how; obtain all the relevant information; concentrate on the pros and cons; then decide.

Once you have made your decision following these rules, Russell counselled, banish the decision from your mind and do not re-open the subject unless *new* information comes to light. If you are sure you originally thought as deeply as you could, don't re-open the subject merely because you are starting to feel uneasy or having second thoughts: that way lies paranoid indecisiveness (and ulcers and stress, Russell might nowadays have added). In five simple steps this is the philosopher's formula – and it works:

1 Obtain all the relevant information
2 Think about the matter as deeply as you know how
3 Make your decision
4 Banish it from your mind unless *new* relevant information comes to light
5 If it does, reconsider the matter, if necessary revise your decision, and then stick by it.

Perhaps you may feel, knowing yourself, that it sounds like an impossibly rigid discipline. It isn't. Try to apply it, and you will find yourself using it all the time after a few weeks.

Finally, on the subject of indecisiveness, we all know of executives who are altogether *too* decisive and most of us act too hastily from time to time because we are in a hurry or in a mood. Nothing said above should be taken to imply that any decision is better than none: far from it. The purpose of Benjamin Franklin's technique, and of all the other suggestions, has been to help you analyse the components of your decisions so you can reach the answer that is right for the situation and right for you.

Most top businessmen view themselves as rather cautious, slow decision-makers. They are not, of course: their skill is to act as rapidly as the circumstances dictate while taking as long to reach their decision as the circumstances allow. In terms of Bertrand Russell's advice, they may well think deeply about a major decision for days or even weeks, knowing that it is more important to be right than to be quick. Bob Jacoby, the dynamic president of the Ted Bates advertising agency, who built Bates into the second largest agency in the world, devised for himself a personal and highly effective combination of action list and decision prompter. He jots down any major decision on a small piece of paper, not just as a note (for example, 'BAM acquisition') but as a question demanding an answer ('If we can't cut the price of the BAM acquisition, should we go ahead?'). He carries a small collection of these notes in his pocket, occasionally draws one out randomly and concentrates on it for a short while. Judging by his decisiveness and his success, it has proved a pretty good system.

Overcoming Laziness

Or do you suspect that you are indecisive and procrastinate because deep down the real you is just, well, lazy? That all these rules and guidelines are fine for people with prolific energy and commitment, but that you are basically indolent at heart, and that's not an ailment which can be cured by rules and guidelines?

In the first place, you cannot be as lazy as all that or you would not be reading *Superefficiency*, and you would certainly not have reached this far if you were not ready, willing and able to improve. Second, the vast majority of truly diligent people – including workaholics – believe themselves to be idlers (because they, far more than real idlers, are intensely aware of how much more they could do if only they tried still harder). So you are probably much less lazy than you fear. Third – and this is the crux of the problem of laziness – unless you literally spend most of your leisure time lying about or asleep, the likelihood is you are as energetic as anyone else but don't release your energies at work.

For example, some years ago I found myself forced to sack a senior executive for idleness over and above the level of acceptability. Naturally I told him why he was being fired and he contested my argument vehemently. He was, he reminded me, a passionate golfer. Most summer evenings he rushed home and played until dark; every morning he was up at dawn to practise until work; at weekends he played eleven or twelve hours each day. So how could I call him lazy?

Yes, he was right, he *wasn't* lazy. Yes, I was right, he *was* lazy at work. In a word, laziness is rarely – as most people believe – a problem of energy; it is a problem of *motivation*. Certainly some people appear to have more energy than others, but 999 times out of 1000 it is their drive rather than their vigour which makes them dynamic. Few of the teenagers who display bored lassitude at the office each day find it difficult to summon up the zest to dance long into the night. So, if you feel yourself to be lazy at work the likelihood, bordering on the certainty, is that you aren't enjoying it much, that you aren't motivated, that you'd sooner be doing something else.

Often the problem is circular: you feel inefficient and indecisive at work, so your subconscious stops you becoming involved, so you lose commitment and drive, so you grow still more inefficient and indecisive . . . If your lack of motivation is the result of such circular causes then *Superefficiency* could well enable you to break the chain by helping you to be more efficient and more decisive.

Usually, however, the problem lies deeper: you are in the wrong job or in the right job in the wrong circumstances (you are at loggerheads with your boss or the company is going through a bad patch or something else is frustrating you). In which case it is decision time, time for an extremely serious pros-and-cons list. Work cannot always be fun (if it were you wouldn't get paid for it!); but if you are finding it so demotivating that it is making you listless and lazy, then something is badly amiss and it may well be time for a change.

Having said all that, only a simpleton in strongly rose-tinted spectacles would suggest that most executives are not a little slothful from time to time; and the best way to minimize such sluggishness as you may be prone to is to set completion dates for major jobs on your master list. Your own completion dates need not, preferably should not, be the same as the organization's. Aim to get things done a day or two before they are needed. That too may sound utopian given the pressure of work, but it isn't. If the chairman ordered the report to be ready two days earlier you would somehow or other get it done. One of the arts of superefficiency is to ensure that your own instructions to yourself carry as much weight as those from the chairman.

> **KEY TIP** Once you've fixed a private completion date for yourself, inform a couple of colleagues by asking if they would kindly be willing to take a quick look at the work when it is done (on your due date, of course). You will then be forced to provide excuses to your colleagues as well as to your conscience if you don't deliver on time.

Facing Unpleasant Situations

One of the most common causes of procrastination is the unwillingness to face unpleasant situations. Typically these are of two kinds:

Telling people they cannot do, or have, something they desperately want
Telling people their performance is unsatisfactory and needs improvement.

We baulk at such confrontations because only the most sadistic and power-crazy executives – of whom there are few, despite naïve novelists' assumptions to the contrary – like to be the cause of unhappiness, and because we get so little practice or training in such situations that we tend to be unsure of our ability to handle them. As a result they become, like going to the dentist, events to be postponed as long as possible. Nowadays most top managers, particularly Americans, recognize this. Hence they see it as part of their job function to chivvy their subordinates into carrying out unpleasant but necessary tasks without undue delay. You will score many career bonus points if you never wait to be chivvied.

Before undertaking such tasks the first essential, too often neglected, is to brief yourself extensively. Almost always the other person will aim to refute your argument and, since the case will be of greater personal interest to him than to you, he will have thought more, and know more, about it. You must have specific details, not generalities, at your fingertips (for example, not 'You are often extremely late back from lunch' but 'You have been more than forty-five minutes late back from lunch nine times in the last four weeks'). If you rely on generalities the argument will get petulant and you will be forced to pull rank.

Once fully briefed you must define the objectives of the confrontation. Presumably – particularly if you are merely rejecting a heartfelt request – you will not want to demotivate the person. On the contrary, you will be keen that he or she accepts what you have to say but does not leave your office utterly downcast and disheartened. This is an exceedingly difficult communication to achieve, but here are some of the ways psychologists' studies have shown it can be done:

Be at pains to be fair Try to hold back, to keep some extra arrows in your quiver; let it be known that you could easily be harder and more critical, but you are sympathetic to their problems and so do not wish to be too harsh.

Criticize actions, not people If you wish them to stay motivated it is vital to avoid undermining their confidence and enthusiasm. Itemize habits and actions, which they can change, not personality traits, which they probably cannot.

Control your non-verbals We've already seen that non-verbal communications often say more than the words we use; this is especially true during criticisms and confrontations, when people are looking for tiny glimmers of reassurance and support. Without minimizing the seriousness of the occasion, smile as often as possible.

Put your remarks in context Refer to the organization's broad philosophy, general rules and regulations or well-known trading situation, so the person can see the logic of your case and accept that it is not a personal attack.

Start with a short and simple statement Anxiety and uncertainty can cause even the most articulate of executives to waffle on such occasions, with disastrous results. As we saw earlier, people find it exceedingly hard to accept and understand criticism, and any lack of clarity can cause utter confusion.

Don't rush Having started with a short and simple statement, it is important to allow sufficient time for the matter to be discussed at length; in particular, for people under fire to feel they have been given ample time to defend themselves.

Seek agreement Without bullying, try hard to get the other person to state his or her agreement, at least generally, to what you have been saying. People who are unwilling to agree in your presence will most certainly leave the room harbouring resentments which will thereafter burgeon like tropical plants in a hothouse.

Encourage suggestions Unless the other person has agreed he will not suggest ways in which his performance can be improved (or he can set about a new project); and he is far more likely to act upon his own suggestions than to accept yours.

Summarize conclusions As such meetings are especially emotional it is crucial to summarize what has been agreed, and what is now going to happen, in a kindly, sympathetic and enthusiastic way.

Finally, when the unhappy event is over, do as Kenneth Blanchard and Spencer Johnson advise in their famous handbook *The One Minute Manager*[11]: stand up, walk with the person to the door, and make a fleeting but encouraging physical contact – putting your arm quickly around the person's shoulders is best. It may sound irksome, but it works wonders on someone who's just been battered about a bit.

Before we reach this chapter's final cause of procrastination, arguments about money, it is worth mentioning one other unpleasant task: firing people.

Many of the guidelines for firing people are similar to those listed above (although you can hardly aim for the person being fired to leave your office other than disheartened):

Be at pains to be fair
Criticize actions not people
Control your non-verbals
Put your remarks in context
Start with a short and simple statement
Don't rush
Seek agreement.

However, there are two additional points about firing people which must forever be kept in mind:

However much they have been expecting to be fired, it always comes as a surprise It is a symptom of human beings' remarkable ability to carry contradictory thoughts in their mind: they know it is going to happen but cannot imagine it actually happening.

After they've gone they will be embittered and consider legal action No matter how apparently reasonable their initial reaction they will soon, understandably, build up a welter of resentment and almost certainly consult their legal advisers. So be extremely cautious not to say anything that might be used in evidence against either you or your organization.

One often hears, in organizations, 'Poor old So and So – he does take criticism badly.' It is almost always uttered by someone who hasn't been criticized lately. I have yet to meet the person who takes criticism well; it is not one of humanity's little foibles. If you keep in mind that it is not eccentric or abnormal to dislike criticism you will learn to handle most unpleasant tasks with humanity, dexterity and without procrastination.

Arguments about Money

A few people relish arguing about money, but most of us dislike it and only do it under sufferance. That is why so many organizations now have separate purchasing departments, which fight about prices even after they have been accepted by the line managers responsible for the purchase. The purchasing departments are staffed by people who have no particular interest in or enthusiasm for the project, have no personal relationship with the supplier and love to haggle. However, with or without a purchasing department, all executives sometimes have to fight about money, and because they dislike doing so such items usually slide backwards down the master list.

As with other unpleasant tasks, bargaining will be less painful if you adhere to some simple disciplines; and as with other unpleasant tasks, it is essential to brief yourself extensively beforehand. If you start to argue about money without being in full possession of the facts you can bet your mark-up to their discount that you'll lose. However, unlike other unpleasant tasks you will be best at it if you treat it as a game: a serious game, which you are determined to win.

Here are some gameplan tactics to help you achieve victory:

Open the bidding If you begin by demanding the price be cut by £10,000, your opponent will feel silly responding with an offer of a few hundred. It is a well-known tactic commonly used by trade unions when wage bargaining.

Pick a nit Even the tiniest nit can, like a hole in a dyke, provide a worthwhile breach in your opponent's case; look for any little pimple which can be inflamed with a deft scratch.

Hang on in there Because the other person is probably at least as embarrassed by the argument as you are, pig-headed perseverance will probably prevail.

Give a little, take a lot Giving away a worthless trinket, to show you are not unreasonable, can help you win the jewel in the crown.

What a larf! American second-hand car dealers are taught to burst out laughing as soon as a car is presented to them for purchase; such belittling chortling can unsettle even the most confident adversary.

Make 'em larf Psychological researchers Karen O'Quin and Joel Aronoff have shown[12] that in financial negotiations you will get a better price if you break down your opponents' defences by making them laugh; it is hard to be hard when you're giggling.

Make 'em compete If you are involved at a sufficiently early stage of the negotiation, gently remind your opponent that there are always other fish in the sea, other pebbles on the beach; a well-timed wink from the green-eyed monster generally works a treat.

Invade their territory Contrary to conventional wisdom, it is almost always advantageous to meet on the other side's turf: they will feel more important, be more relaxed, thus be more susceptible to your wiles; and if they aren't, it will be easier for you to stomp out.

Having discussed tactics, a few words on style. When arguing about money, should you be aggressive or firmly conciliatory? At Harvard Professor Roger Fisher and William Ury, probably the most experienced negotiation researchers in the world, have defined the two styles thus[13]:

Conciliatory	*Aggressive*
Participants are friendly; the goal is agreement	Participants are adversaries; the goal is victory
Make concessions to cultivate relationship	Demand concessions as a condition of the relationship
Be soft on the people and the problem	Be hard on the people and the problem
Trust others	Distrust others
Change your position easily	Dig into your position
Make offers	Make threats
Disclose your bottom line	Mislead as to your bottom line
Accept one-sided losses to reach agreement	Demand one-sided gains as the price of agreement
Search for the single answer: the one they will accept	Search for the single answer: the one you will accept
Insist on agreement	Insist on your position
Try to avoid a contest of will	Try to win a contest of will
Yield to pressure	Apply pressure

The purpose of separating these two opposing styles of negotiation, as we saw with tigers and foxes when assessing different styles of salesmanship, is to show that neither is uniquely and universally right. Which you employ will depend both upon your personality and upon whether the dispute is a single, once-and-for-all event or part of a continuous relationship. Most negotiation pundits agree that you can afford to be more aggressive in single-occasion negotiations than in continuing associations.

However, Fisher and Ury's principal contribution to the art of financial negotiation is the BATNA. The BATNA is the 'Best Alternative To a Negotiated Agreement'. It is your fallback position which in any important financial battle you should have defined beforehand. As Fisher and Ury put it:

> Vigorous exploration of what you will do if you do not reach agreement can greatly strengthen your hand. Attractive alternatives are not just sitting there waiting for you; you usually have to develop them. Generating possible BATNAs requires distinct operations: (1) inventing a list of actions you might conceivably take if no agreement is reached; (2) improving some of the more promising ideas and converting them into practical options; and (3) selecting, tentatively, the one option that seems best.

To start developing BATNAs before negotiations begin will seem unduly pessimistic to naïve enthusiasts: 'Get stuck-in, confident you'll win' is their battlecry. Balderdash. In negotiations overbuoyant optimism is always asinine. 'The better your BATNA the greater your power' according to Fisher and Ury, and having developed BATNAs ever since I first learned of the system I'll second that.

Developing BATNAs is one of the gameplan tactics which – along with opening the bidding, making 'em larf, invading their territory and the rest – will help you expunge your embarrassment about arguing about money. Indeed, with their help you should quickly become so proficient at the game that you'll keep winning, and maybe even surprise yourself by coming to enjoy it.

Nobody of intelligence would pretend it is easy to defeat procrastination; indeed, nobody of intelligence would claim it is possible for human beings – no matter how superefficient – utterly to eradicate procrastination from their lives. From the lowliest employee to the grandest chairman and chief executive, we all procrastinate occasionally, as well as lazing about during working hours from time to time. Equally, as we saw at the beginning of the chapter, we are all extraordinarily decisive in innumerable ordinary ways.

So the difference between the superefficient and everyone else is not one of kind but one of degree; and the logical corollary is that you can easily learn to prioritize, become more decisive, overcome idleness and deal with unpleasant tasks if you face the situation and diligently decide to view prioritization as a priority.

4

HOW TO
DOMINATE DATA

Data management is one of the most rapidly developing aspects of modern life, growing daily more sophisticated and specialized. And *Superefficiency* is not – as by now will have become self-evident – intended for the specialist. So this is not a chapter written for data processing managers and office automation consultants. It is, like the rest of the book, designed to help the nonspecialist cope with, and master, the escalating mass of reports and computer sheets, sales analyses and financial projections which nowadays choke up every in-tray, every briefcase and every executive's mind, endangering the very survival of unfettered creative thought.

The Paper Jungle

'A man's best friend is his wastepaper basket' quipped the magazine *Business Week* some years ago, and that maxim encapsulates one of business life's eternal verities: like every good executive, every piece of paper should have a home to go to. So why is it that most executives' desks are chock-a-block with homeless quires of stationery? It is simply because too many executives have failed to take a machete to the paper jungle.

As we mentioned when discussing procrastination, some aspects of superefficiency are difficult, or even impossible, to master completely. But there is no excuse for allowing yourself to get trapped in the paper jungle. The proof: many companies insist that every executive leaves a clear desk each night, and in no time at all new employees learn to abide by the rule, without going on a lengthy training course or suffering a traumatic mental breakdown in the process.

As it happens, leaving a clear desk each night is no proof of superefficiency. (Indeed, the brilliant chief executive of one of the most successful Japanese companies operating in Britain is highly suspicious of scrupulously clear desks: he suspects they mean that not a lot is happening.) In order to obey the clean-desk rule some executives simply stuff any loose papers into a desk drawer each night, and then waste time sorting them out each morning. That's not the way to do it.

The way to do it is to apply the precept that every piece of paper should have a home to go to by developing a parking system for sifting and sorting your papers. The best is the 6-D parking system:

Starting from the bottom, and agreeing with *Business Week*, you can probably dump many of the documents that come across your desk with no risk whatsoever; and you must, because unless you do so those few that are vital and important will get lost in a morass of junk.

Question whether you are likely ever to refer to the document again; question whether nobody else will file it; question whether anything dreadful would result from its demise. Unless you get a positive yes from two of these three queries, dump it.

Much of what you cannot dump you can, and should, delay. These are not procrastinating postponements but deliberate delays, to avoid each newly arrived piece of paper forcing you to skip haphazardly from subject to subject. Put aside unimportant letters and memos; long documents which you will need to study thoughtfully in tranquillity; junk advertising mail which you wish to cast a quick eye over when you've a spare moment; trade magazines after you've skip-read the headlines; and computer sheets which call for careful, but non-urgent, analysis.

But 'put aside' does not mean pile in a higgledy-piggledy, disorderly heap on your desk. You can only park these documents correctly if you have a series of 'parking lots' designed for the purpose: a stack of filing trays or hanging files in a deep desk drawer are ideal.

KEY TIP Keep your briefcase open by your desk and put straight into it any documents, like reports and trade magazines, destined to be read overnight. There is no point in first putting such documents into a pending tray, as many executives do, and then wasting time each evening going through the pending tray again before depositing them in your briefcase.

A particularly useful form of delay file, often called a 'tickler' file, is a concertina file with thirty-one (or a few more) sections, each of which is numbered for a day of the month, 1st-31st. (If you handle an especially vast volume of paper you may need thirty-one individual files, but a concertina file is far easier to use.)

You then write on the document the date when you intend to deal with it and park it in the tickler file, or ask your secretary to do so. Every morning, or better still every previous evening, you or your secretary checks the file to see which documents are due to be dealt with on that day. The system, which is virtually foolproof, can be used to carry documents forward several months. Say it is 31 January and you write 15 April on the document, then deposit it in the 15th section. You will see it on 15

February, 15 March – which will remind you of its existence – before it eventually comes up for action in April.

Once you get a tickler file working efficiently you can write notes to yourself, date them, and rely on them coming back to you on the date specified. Incidentally, a personal computer, if you have one, can be an ideal tickler file.

Returning to the 6-D parking system, we have now dealt with documents to be dumped and delayed and can turn to documents which can be delegated.

Inevitably many of the papers that reach your desk should immediately be diverted to somebody more appropriate to deal with them. However, it is always wise to keep a note of such documents, since there is a fair chance you will find yourself held responsible if the person to whom you've passed them does not deal with them expeditiously.

For greater efficiency still you should aim to delegate as much paperwork as possible before it reaches your desk. An intelligent secretary can obviously be an excellent filter (though it is equally important for *her* to note any documents she passes on to others against the possibility of future queries).

In addition, you should 'delegate' by removing your name from as many distribution lists as possible. To those responsible for distributing trade magazines, government reports, minutes of meetings and a host of other dossiers it seems, rather puzzlingly, to be a matter of pride and prestige for their lists to be peopled with casts of thousands. Perhaps they feel it makes their work worthwhile; and perhaps that's why you will find them so reluctant to let you escape once one of their lists has ensnared you. Still, their problems aren't your problems. Delegate the reading of worthy but mundane documents to others whenever you can, and ask them to send you only extracts and precis personally relevant to you.

By now you will have hacked away most of the paper jungle, leaving only those documents which you must 'Do' – documents you must attend to more or less immediately. To some of these you will be able to write or dictate immediate answers: to some you will be able to send standard, prewritten replies (see Chapter 1); but for many you will need to obtain additional information before you can deal with them.

Put in hand the acquisition of this information by telephone or memo immediately; then consign the documents to a 'Do' or action file, which should be like a transit camp – or the lifts in a multi-storey car park – where things never stay for long before moving to their destination. Remember that every piece of paper should have a home to go to; the Do file is only for short stopovers.

Finally, in our less than utopian real world, there will always be papers which arrive on our desks which cannot neatly be parked in the 6-D system; papers posing problems we are uncertain how to solve. Such awkward documents can either be stored in the Do file, where you know they will keep rearing their bothersome heads, or in their own special file (which you might call a 'ticklish', instead of a 'tickler', file).

As with unpleasant tasks, you must force yourself to deal with such documents without too much delay, since it's a safe bet they will precipitate you into the mire if you don't. And the best way to spur yourself into action is to mark the document with a red dot each time you look at it but fail to take action. Allow three red dots to accumulate but no more. The fourth time you look at the document, do nothing else until you have decided how to deal with it and initiated any necessary action. Otherwise you will inevitably procrastinate indefinitely (and end up in the mire).

KEY TIP When it isn't vital to send a typed letter scribble a brief (but legible!) reply on incoming correspondence, get a photostat for your records and send the original back again.

Filing

Once again we are here considering your own personal filing, and not the company filing or your office filing, which should be the responsibility of others. But every efficient executive needs a small set of important, frequently used, often confidential, files close to hand. And the operative word is 'small'. Following the advice given above I have, throughout my career, chucked away most documents once they have been read, relying upon other people to file their copies: it has never yet caused even the glimmer of a problem. As a result my personal filing cabinets have always been small and sparsely populated. The corollary of which is that I can usually remember exactly which documents are in them and can find them quickly.

In contrast, we have all watched executives plough through innumerable folders and reams of paper, searching through overcrowded cabinets and drawer after drawer, only to finish up defeated and despairing because the papers they remember putting carefully away somewhere cannot be found anywhere. If you are not going to be able to find a document it is far better not to find it quickly.

The construction of an efficient filing system is dependent on the categorization of the files. Most filing systems contain a fair number of sections that are empty or hold only a single sheet of paper, and another group of sections that are bulging full to overflowing. This means that whoever set up the system did not consider carefully the categorizations.

The function of a filing system is not storage but retrieval. If you keep that in mind when defining and titling the sections, you should succeed in designing a superefficient system. The fact that it is your own personal system means that the titles need not mean much to anyone else (designing a system for others is a great deal harder).

Whether you file alphabetically by customer, or alphabetically by project, or numerically by job number, or whatever, will depend on the nature of your work.

Whichever you choose, remember that the titling or categorization is the essence of the system: unless it is simple, clear and meaningful (to you) you will never be certain which section to put things into or, an inexorable consequence, into which section you put things.

Finally, three additional points which will make your filing function more effectively:

Cross-references Computers, of course, are the ideal tools for cross-referencing, but in your own small way you can emulate them if you train yourself always to scribble potentially useful cross-references on every document, while they are fresh in your mind, before you file the document; doing so will save you aeons of time later on.

Colour coding Use different coloured files to separate subjects or projects or years.

Spring-cleaning However busy you are, at least once a year you must whistle through the entire system and dump all the documents that have become obsolete. If you have not allowed the files to become overweight by stuffing them too full, it will take no more than a couple of hours at the most. It will inevitably also serve the subsidiary purpose of reminding you of two or three things which you had forgotten but which now seem worth reviving.

Read Less More Efficiently

On average people read approximately 200 words per minute and retain about 40 per cent of what they read. If you go on a speed reading course you can increase your rate to 600 words per minute and your retention score to 70 per cent. Unfortunately, experience has shown that unless you continuously force yourself to keep in training by using the special speed reading techniques you will slowly slip back to your normal speed and retention levels. This doubtless explains why speed reading courses, all the rage in the 1960s and early 1970s, are no longer so fashionable.

However, several of the basic techniques of speed reading can be invaluable to every executive who feels there is more paperwork to peruse than there are minutes in the day. First, and most important, learn to skim.

When you enter a room your eyes and brain take in an overall, general impression of the contents without assimilating the detail. After you've been in the room a few minutes you will have absorbed much more of the detail, especially things of particular interest or relevance to you: a photograph of someone you know perhaps, or furniture similar to your own, or curtaining material you saw in a shop at a knock-down price. No matter how observant you are, you will not see – or at least will not consciously see – every single detail of the room (every stitch in the upholstery, every speck of dust) because that would be, quite literally, impossible.

The formula for effective skim reading is much the same. When you first receive a report or document whizz through it to obtain an overall general impression of the contents without trying to assimilate the detail. Then go fairly quickly through it again, allowing your eyes to linger over any words or phrases that seem relevant and important; the human eye/brain mechanism is unbelievably quick at spotting words and numbers that have particular relevance to them. (Have you ever noticed how your own name seems to jump out at you from the page of a newspaper? Similarly, this is the reason why you will notice even a tiny advertisement headlined 'Stomach Cramps' if you happen to be suffering.)

By now you will know which parts of the document need to be read carefully (if any; many documents get consigned to the bin at this point) and which parts can be ignored. Mark those that demand further study either with a transparent magic marker or with a soft pencil in the margin. Of course, if you are a lawyer and the document is a legal contract you must pore over every word because that is your job. But such situations are the exception rather than the rule: we all know that most documents we read contain little that is very important and many contain nothing at all.

If you wish to read still more quickly, here are two more hints from speed reading courses:

Use a pointer   In the same way that children use a finger to help them along the line, use a pencil or a ruler beneath the line and move it quickly. It takes a little practice, but studies have shown that the use of a pointer can increase your reading speed by as much as 100 per cent while also improving comprehension, understanding and memory.

Reduce subvocalization   Pronouncing the words silently to yourself, or 'subvocalization' as psychologists call it, is probably the greatest impediment to fast reading. The way to stop doing it is to start humming while you read; eventually you'll begin to read, without subvocalizing the words, by sight instead of sound (and you will, you'll be pleased to read, be able to stop the humming).

Obviously the effortless way to increase the speed of your reading is, as you have already read in the section on paperwork, to get other people to do your reading for you, preferably people who are either specialists in the subject – for example, lawyers, accountants, market researchers – or your subordinates, who can expect a fair rollicking if they fail to draw your attention to any significant item of which you ought to be appraised.

Likewise, erasing your name from unnecessary distribution lists will increase the speed with which you read those documents, so to speak, infinitely. However, in your admirable and understandable determination to read less more efficiently you must take care to avoid throwing the baby out with the bathwater. (You'd hardly expect the author of a fine, old-fashioned, printed book to suggest otherwise!)

A deft way to deal with thick business magazines of the *Fortune* and *Forbes* type, devised by Christopher Collins, the dynamic chairman of Bibendum Wines, is to skim through the contents list and select the one – and only one

– article you most wish to read. Don't allow yourself to be seduced into reading any more, no matter how succulent the other article may look, or you will soon find yourself with back issues choking up your in-tray again (you still haven't read that other article which looked so fascinating in last December's issue so there's no point in moving on . . .) and eventually you'll cancel your subscription in frustration.

Finally, here are some rules which will make the reading that is unavoidable easier and the likelihood of retention greater:

Maintain good posture   It's acceptable to read with your feet propped on your desk, but don't expect fast reading rates in that position; poor posture impedes circulation and concentration drops. It is best to read sitting upright in a straight-backed chair with the document 15-24 inches in front of you at a 45-degree angle, with all points equidistant from your eyes.

Avoiding the morning after   If you know you've lots of reading in store, don't drink too much the night before. It doesn't just *seem* more difficult to read with a hangover, it *is* more difficult. Alcohol impairs your vision while you are imbibing (drinking doubles usually means seeing doubles) and thereafter.

Schedule reading time   The most timewasting and irritating way of reading is under the pressure of constant interruptions: you lose your place, lose the thread of the argument, lose your memory of the last sentence, and lose your temper. If you have a hefty tome to read, then block the time out in your diary and brook no interruptions. That way your brain will know you mean business and concentrate willingly on its work.

Get the ambience right   Don't leave papers all over the desk as they are likely to distract the eye. Don't try to read in bad light (we all do so from time to time and it is ludicrously dumb). Don't have the temperature too high –

temperatures above 18° C (70° F) are soporific and not conducive to concentration.

Relax your eyes During extended reading periods, if you occasionally look up and focus on distant objects you will relax your eye muscles, which will help you to carry on reading without fatigue. Alternatively, 'palming' your eyes by closing them and cupping them with your hand to produce total blackness will provide them with a valuable moment of relaxation and rest.

Finally, if you are involved in an especially protracted reading session, perhaps all morning or all day, and if you have any privacy in your office, or even in the washroom, indulge yourself in a few easy physical exercises – touching your toes and cycling your arms. This will improve circulation and thus concentration. The Japanese practice of giving employees 'physical jerks' breaks isn't altruistic; the companies are well aware that by thus benefiting their workers they benefit themselves.

Here's to the Memory

Using your memory as effectively as possible is one of the fundamentals of superefficiency. Yet while the quantity of data with which we have to deal increases seemingly exponentially each year, the ability of our memories to cope with it steadily decreases. Learning ability decreases from our teens and early twenties onwards, and memories start to lose their edge from our early forties.

If your memory is marvellous and you are never absent-minded, you can skip this section: you don't need it. If you are less certain about your memory, you can resolve the question by completing this brief self-assessment questionnaire:

	Once a month or more	Several times in a year	Never
Score:	*(3)*	*(2)*	*(1)*

1 Do you forget where you parked the car?

2 Do you forget birthdays, anniversaries, important meetings or other special occasions?

3 Do you go shopping and return without the item you went to buy?

4 Do you ask people to return your calls and then forget why you called them in the first place?

5 Do you do one thing while thinking of something else?

6 Do you leave the house to go somewhere and have to return for something you forgot?

7 Do you put things in the wrong places, like your keys in the refrigerator and the milk in the cupboard?

8 Do you lose your train of thought?

9 Do you do something more than once because you forgot you did it in the first place?

10 Do you become so absorbed in thought that you lose awareness of your surroundings?

Total score	*Assessment*
0-10	Congratulations! Your memory is so good you could give an elephant fair competition, and you can certainly skip this section.
11-20	Your memory is pretty good, but could easily be helped and improved; you are probably suffering somewhat from the strains of a busy life. You ought to read on.
21-30	You are becoming quite absent-minded and forgetful; but you can minimize your forgetfulness if you train your memory with some of the following suggestions. You should definitely read on.

Incidentally, if you know that you lead an exceedingly busy life, do not be too alarmed if the test shows your memory to be marginally worse than you believe it to be. Statistics produced by memory researchers have shown that the greater the number of situations in which memory lapses are possible, the greater the number of memory lapses that will occur. In other words, the more you need to remember the more you will forget.

Memory being one of the most complex, vital and fascinating of humanity's faculties, over recent years it has been the subject of much scientific research. The researchers have established that memory is not a single, homogeneous function but a complex interaction of different functions – long-term memory, subdivided into episodic and semantic memories; short-term memory; sensory memory, or iconic memory as it is sometimes called, subdivided into auditory, visual and other sensory memories; haptic memory, which combines sensory and spatial memories, to make it possible, for example, to play musical instruments. As the scientists' researches advance, doubtless many new classifications of memory will be discovered.

The researchers have also established that inside our heads we possess a system for classifying, storing and retrieving information that is superior in capacity, flexibility and speed not only to any computer that exists, but to any computer than can be dreamed of.

Here's a simple test to prove the point. Do you know the word 'diggleflinch'? No? Hardly surprising, as it doesn't exist. How long did it take you to realize you didn't know the word? You knew instantaneously. A suitably programmed computer would have had to check every word in its memory and establish *negatively* that there was no such word; your memory did the same thing *positively*, instantly. The mystery is that although you know you don't know 'diggleflinch', you probably cannot remember whether you definitely sent that letter yesterday to Jim Duggleflunch, or even, like Nathan Detroit in *Guys and Dolls*, the colour of the tie you are now wearing.

Unhappily, but perhaps unsurprisingly, current research evidence suggests that you cannot literally change your total power of memory. None the less there is no doubt that you can train your memory to be more effective, as young actors do when they learn to learn lines. The following recommendations, then, offer you ways to use your memory to greatest effect, to help you memorize the things you need to, instead of the profusion of inconsequential flotsam that your mind seems so to enjoy collecting when left to its own devices.

The first and most crucial advice, which has already cropped up again and again, is to take the strain off your brain by devising simple routines which allow your brain to remember one thing instead of many. That is the basic purpose of diaries and master lists, of decision analyses and tickler files: you merely remember to do one thing – look at the master list – and then your eyes take over from your memory. And if you can turn the action into a routine habit – looking at the master list each morning should become as habitual as putting on your shoes – then another burden is lifted from your memory's shoulders.

The more you can lighten its load, the research evidence indicates, the more successfully will your memory cope with the rest of its tasks, so you'll be able to minimize your forgetfulness and absent-mindedness.

Absent-mindedness comprises three categories of forgetfulness:

Forgetting where you put things
Forgetting forthcoming events
Forgetting what you're doing at the moment.

To aid your memory further, let's consider each in turn.

FORGETTING WHERE YOU PUT THINGS

You'll be more likely to remember where you put things if you:

Have a parking space for everything   As we saw earlier, that is the function of filing systems (retrieval not storage), but it can be adopted in innumerable aspects of your working life, with significant timesaving benefits.

Make visual associations   Tying memory strands together is one of the principal methods of memory improvement. When you park your car, look for something odd or unusual nearby; when you leave your coat, try to remember the colour of the cloakroom attendant's eyes, and so on.

Retrace events   Mentally retracing what you did in the few minutes before the item went missing will often help jog your memory as to where you put it.

Put things together   Put things you might forget, like papers for a meeting, next to something you cannot forget, like your coat in winter; or on a train put something you might lose, like a scarf, on top of or in the pocket of your jacket.

Put things where you can't miss them   Balance letters on the doorknob, or pile books in the doorway, or hang files from your desk lamp with tape – in other words, place essential things in incongruous positions where you cannot possibly overlook them.

Many of the aids to remembering events and appointments have already been mentioned – diaries, master lists, tickler files and the rest – but here are several more:

Have a daily schedule Write out for yourself each morning or, better still, have your secretary type that day's appointments on a separate piece of paper, together with anything special you need to do or remember in connection with each appointment. For example, '3.30 meeting with Sales Director, remember to take last *two* years' sales figures'. Always carry the paper with you; you'll soon get used to referring to it throughout the day.

Notes on the mirror If you are not going straight to work in the morning, write a note the night before and stick it on the bathroom mirror.

Knots in the handkerchief The old joke, 'I tied a knot in my handkerchief to remind myself and now I can't remember why I tied it', is precisely that: an old joke. Putting knots in your handkerchief or large pieces of paper in your pocket or anything equivalent are all quick and reliable memory joggers.

Carry a notepad Many busy and efficient people carry notepads everywhere and frequently consult them; you can buy them handsomely leather-bound or cheap and cheerful. Alternatively some people prefer cards, about 8 × 3 inches, which are firm enough to write on; they can be obtained from most stationers.

FORGETTING WHAT YOU ARE DOING

This is the hardest type of absent-mindedness to alleviate because it creeps up on you subconsciously. The most effective way to beat it is to fight it: don't resign yourself to becoming more absent-minded; don't excuse yourself by muttering, 'Einstein was dreadfully absent-minded and he was a genius'; make a conscious commitment to be more aware and chastise yourself when you fail.

To achieve this, it helps if you force yourself to live in the present. Think about what is happening now rather than worrying about something in the future or something you've already done. This is especially important when you should be listening (Chapter 1, 'Be attentive').

Your memory is like a muscle: it needs to be stretched and exercised to keep it in peak condition but, again like muscle, it will tire if it's overused. It doesn't like alcohol, or too much caffeine or too little blood sugar – all of which promote forgetfulness (and often, in the case of excess alcohol, total amnesia). But if you cosset your memory in the ways suggested it will serve you superefficiently until well beyond your retirement.

KEY TIP   Forgetting people's names – one of the most universal of memory problems – will be minimized if you adopt the American habit of repeating their names loudly when you are introduced: 'Hello, Mr Duggleflunch, it's good to meet you', instead of the traditionally more reticent British 'Good morning'.

Computer Crunching

If *Superefficiency* is revised and republished in 2001 AD this section will probably be the longest in the book. That is not because the inefficiencies that humanity is heir to will disappear. Many executives will still communicate badly, waste too much time, postpone unpleasant tasks, be indecisive and forgetful. Those qualities (qualities?) are as inherent in humanity as breathing and sleeping, and computers won't change them.

But by 2001 AD most executives will have a personal

computer or mainframe terminal on their desk and will use it continuously. Today, despite the microcomputer revolution that has occurred since 1975, few keyboards and VDUs are to be seen on desktops outside those specialist departments which use them all the time: finance, research, data processing, sales administration and stock control.

More significantly still, the number of minis and micros being bought by small businesses is surging ahead, although recent research suggests that a depressingly large proportion of them still aren't used properly or fully, and many end up gathering dust in the storeroom within weeks of being bought.

Computerization, in all its many aspects, is developing so rapidly that the problems it causes today will be solved tomorrow. None the less, the superefficient executive will always need to keep the following in mind in his relationships with those mindless brains of the future:

GIGO The oldest and best-known rule about computers is 'garbage in garbage out', yet despite its fame most executives still imbue computer data with unimpeachable sanctity. Don't. Question it relentlessly. Computers don't think, they regurgitate other people's thoughts, and those people may well have made mistakes.

Too much is too much Some years ago in the USA General Motors instituted an advertising effectiveness study which sought to correlate advertising with monthly sales in every area of that vast country. The resulting volume of data was so enormous, the computer sheets so weighty, that the executives handling the project could hardly cope. A recurrent theme of *Superefficiency* has been to avoid undertaking too much: don't let the computer beat you, even if it is bigger than you.

Perfect the printout In most organizations a fair number of the computer printouts are far from perfect. They contain too much data or too little, or the right data wrongly analysed. Often the format was fine when it was first designed, but hasn't been changed for a couple of years; often each executive thinks it must be fine for somebody else, whereas it is really wrong for everyone. Don't waste time wrestling with imperfect printouts: get them put right and everyone will thank you.

Wordprocessors are wonderful   If your organization has a wordprocessing department, make full use of it; alternatively get a wordprocessor for your secretary; alternatively learn to use one yourself. They make document redrafting, duplicating and simple retrieval a billion times easier (at least!).

Don't minimize, maximize   As mentioned earlier, many computer users fail to exploit their computer's full powers and use only a few of the functions. This is understandable at the start, but plain foolish once the simple functions have been mastered. Check that you are using your equipment to the full.

Train back-up staff   All too often in small companies only one person, or at the most two, knows how to use the computer, so whenever that person is away the computer takes an expensive snooze. Make sure at least three or four people know the rudiments of its operation sufficiently to keep it operating.

Ergonomics are more important than economics   'User friendly' is a terminological inexactitude invented by the computer industry because its products aren't. Unless your computer is relatively pleasant and comfortable to use, somehow or other people (including you) will avoid using it.

Software is more important than hardware   The mechanical differences between the leading makes of computer are now little more significant than the chemical differences between leading brands of detergent. The important differences lie in the range, cost and variety of software available. Check there are inexpensive and flexible software programs available which will meet your particular needs.

Service is more important than everything All computers, like all other machines (including – not here, irrelevantly – human machines), go wrong occasionally. Once you have integrated a computer into your operation this can be disastrous: work may literally come to a standstill, as anyone who has suffered computer failure at an airport check-in desk well knows. It is crucial to ensure that reliable service and repair resources are available instantly and always. Check very carefully in advance; later it will be too late.

Believe! Believe! The most common reason for computers not being used properly or fully or at all is that they have been acquired by people searching for a simple saviour to solve some problems, but lacking a total commitment to computerization. If you acquire a computer it will involve you in changing some of your other systems; maybe in changing some of your people; definitely in changing some of the ways you work. Unless you are committed, these changes won't occur, and you'll be lucky to sell the saviour for scrap.

Remember that computers don't make decisions, humans do. As computers have grown more ubiquitous it has become dismally common to hear executives try to explain away foolish decisions by saying 'The computer showed . . .' or 'Our computer analyses proved . . .' Fiddlesticks, gobbledygook and GIGO. Obviously you were right to obtain all the relevant data the computer had in its innards; but the decision, buddy, was yours.

Computers, as we said at the outset, do not think; less still do they come up with brilliant and original ideas; but you must, if you are to be superefficient and supersuccessful. So let's now consider how you can increase your output of winning ideas.

5

IDEAS, IDEAS

Nobody gets to be successful – no matter how efficient and thorough they become – by doing things the way they have always been done before. That's why the fifth key to *superefficiency* is learning to solve problems in new ways by having winning ideas.

How can you spur yourself into having winning ideas? People believe ideas come like bolts from the blue – most often, according to traditional mythology, when you are in the bath – causing you to leap out, cry 'Eureka', and announce to a waiting world or the bathroom mirror the birth of a notion.

That may be traditional mythology but it isn't how Archimedes discovered his principle, or how Einstein discovered relativity, or – despite the famous falling apple – how Newton discovered gravity. Each of them had long been pondering the problem, mulling it over in his mind, struggling to find a solution which fitted the facts. Genius is an infinite capacity for taking pains or, as Thomas Edison – himself no mean hand at inventions – said: 'Genius is 1 per cent inspiration and 99 per cent perspiration.' So before getting to the inspiration we had better tackle the perspiration.

Analysing Problems

It is a truism to say that you cannot come up with the right answers unless you ask the right questions; but when the problem lies in having ideas, it is a truism often ignored. We all know people who throw off bright ideas like sparks from Catherine wheels; but, like the sparks, their ideas quickly die. Why?

It is almost always because the ideas do not quite solve the problem in hand. Sometimes they are impractical; more often they are not quite relevant, because nobody has defined the problem sufficiently carefully. Not that it is always easy to define problems: on the contrary, the acute and perceptive analysis of problems is a rare skill, and frequently the exact definition of a problem will of itself reveal the solution.

Genius is 99 per cent perspiration because the understanding and defining of complex problems is itself a creative act. Automobile manufacturers all knew that cars can be produced in a multiplicity of colours; it took Henry Ford to see that costs would be reduced and mass demand generated if they were manufactured in one colour only: black. Was that a brilliant solution? Or was it a brilliant analysis of the problem? It doesn't matter. The two were inextricably intertwined; they frequently are.

At work we are rarely handed clearly defined problems. Most commonly we face situations where something is wrong and we need to identify what it is. That is a *mess* problem. Alternatively, things seem to be running smoothly and efficiently, yet we know they could – with new equipment or a different system – run still more smoothly, still more efficiently. That is an *improvement* problem. For most of us the 80/20 principle applies: 80 per cent of our problems are messes, 20 per cent improvements.

It should be your constant aim to reverse that balance. Part of the purpose of *Superefficiency* is to help you do so. One of the paramount reasons for becoming superefficient is to whittle away the messes, muddles and mistakes which normally take up so much of your time, leaving you free to concentrate on the improvements and developments which – as well as being more productive – are a great deal more satisfying and fun.

However, whether you are facing a mess or an improvement problem, the five steps involved in its analysis are broadly similar:

1. PUT THE PROBLEM IN PERSPECTIVE

Most of the problems executives face, particularly mess problems, appear to be narrow and specific: should I fire Mary? Why did the delivery arrive late? Can the showcards be reprinted in time? How come the computer data is garbage? Before tackling the specific snag which, of course, you must do speedily – consider carefully whether it is a symptom of a wider problem. Otherwise, when you've solved the immediate headache, you will move on to other urgent matters, and as sure as broken eggs are broken eggs a similar difficulty will occur, generated by the same root cause. Then it will be too late, and you will kick yourself for having failed to give the matter sufficient attention in the first place.

2. STATE THE PROBLEM PRECISELY

If the problem is of any significance at all you should write it down: as always, writing will clarify your thoughts. Still more important, you should boil the problem down to one sentence – two at the most. Unless you can define it concisely you will not have identified the problem clearly. You will be waffling. And if you have not identified the problem clearly, clearly you cannot expect to solve it.

Alternatively, if – despite trying hard – the issue cannot be shrunk into one sentence, it may be that you have unearthed a morass of interwoven troubles, in which case you need to break the whole lot down into specific subproblems.

You should also, at this stage of the analysis, start to be creative. Don't state the problem as a well-worn cliché; if your statement of the problem is old-hat, it is likely your solution will be likewise.

3. SPECIFY THE OBJECTIVES

The objectives should arise almost logically from your statement of the problem and ought again to be written down as succinctly and clearly as you know how. From now on everything you do must be judged against this statement of objectives: it will be the only accurate way to assess whether or not you've succeeded at the end of the day. So consider carefully whether you have set yourself

(a) sufficiently broad objectives (see step 1 above)
(b) sufficiently challenging objectives
(c) achievable objectives.

Only when you have satisfied yourself on all three counts should you move on to step 4.

4. GET THE FACTS

All too often people start to collect facts before they know which facts will be relevant. Inevitably they are influenced by the facts they have collected, and they bend their vision of the problem and its solution to their new prejudices.

To help you realize how exceptionally difficult it is to assess facts fairly, think of the highly formalized and regulated way in which facts ('evidence') are presented in courts of law. The statement of the problem (the charge) and the objectives (guilty or not guilty) are dealt with in minutes, but the presentation, analysis and questioning of the facts (the hearing of the case) can stretch out interminably. And the rules governing which types of statement are acceptable, which not, have been honed and refined over centuries, to try to ensure that they do not sway the magistrate or jury unfairly.

It isn't too fanciful to say that the collection and assessment of facts should always be subject to the same stringent attempts at objectivity. Nothing more frequently leads executives to false conclusions than obtaining too few facts or irrelevant facts or the wrong facts. And misleading facts get stuck in the mind like burrs (again as courts well know: jurists never disregard a statement merely because the judge has ordered them to do so).

So the rules about getting the facts are:

Don't rush in: make sure you know what you're looking for

If a dispute is involved, make sure you hear both sides of it (plus evidence from uninvolved witnesses wherever possible)

Be thorough: don't give up when you seem to have enough data to support your point of view (or justify your prejudices)

Make sure you take full cognizance of any facts which challenge your point of view

If necessary, and if time and money allow, obtain further data, through research, which will help clarify the issues.

Sadly, however assiduous you are, you will almost never obtain all the facts you think you need, and to delay solving a problem on this account is yet another, unacceptable, form of procrastination.

5. POSTULATE VARIOUS SOLUTIONS

Step 5 is the bridge between analysing the problem and generating the idea or ideas which will solve it. If you reach step 5 and cannot rapidly draft some possible courses of action with little effort – and don't worry at this point about being original: originality will re-enter the process later – then something has probably gone badly awry earlier.

You undertook steps 1 to 4 to help you find the best, most creative solution to the problem. If you cannot postulate *any* solutions then step 4 has proved a dead end. It's back to the drawing board, I'm afraid.

Before leaving the subject of problem analysis, it is

important briefly to list those factors which, as psychologists have established, often block and blinker our logical thought processes, leading us to distorted views and unreasonable conclusions:

Resistance to change   Everybody suffers some fear of change, since change brings with it the unknown, but it is vital to keep such anxieties under strict control. In today's economy it is change that makes the world go around.

Over-reliance on others   While it is never wrong to seek advice, some people cannot resolve problems because they have drifted into a state of utter reliance on others. Unfortunately, such a malaise will eventually incapacitate the person completely and then psychological or psychiatric help may be required.

I've been there before   We have tried to guard against this blinker by stressing the importance of originality in steps 2 and 3. None the less, we are all prone to jump to conclusions when faced with a predicament which seems exactly like a previous one. Sometimes we are right to do so, but frequently 'I've been there before' stops us taking a fresh and unprejudiced view of the situation.

Cultural blocks   This is perhaps the most difficult blinker to throw off, because cultural norms have been inculcated into us since birth and influence almost everything we do; nor is it always possible or sensible to seek solutions which contradict cultural norms. On the other hand, saying 'That's the way it's always been done' guarantees sterility. It is frequently necessary to be radical, but rarely to be revolutionary.

Low motivation   A lack of real interest in the problem leads to a search for the easy way out and the path of least resistance; it leads to a disregard for the facts and sloppy thinking. We all see it happening at work every day and it leads to more disasters than most of us have mislaid memos.

Overstrong motivation This is the converse of low motivation and is less common, but is equally certain to lead to havoc. When we are too emotionally involved with a problem we take every setback and criticism personally, bias the facts, misinterpret results, act hastily and dwell obsessively on the consequences of failure, none of which constitutes an ideal prescription for calm, rational thought.

Creativity

Brain specialists have long known that the brain is divided into two halves, left and right. But it was the pioneering work of Professor Robert Ornstein at the University of California in the 1960s which established that the two halves operate quite differently, and indeed almost separately, from each other[14].

Having established that the two halves of the brain are biologically similar, Ornstein realized that they can more realistically be thought of as two independent brains working in harmony than as a single brain divided into two, because each half-brain carries out different functions, functions that the other half-brain has no idea how to perform.

In general the left-hand brain handles 'logical' thinking, the right-hand brain 'creative' thinking:

Brain functions

Left	Right
Mathematics	Imagination
Language	Colour
Analysis	Music
Deduction	Rhythm
Logic	Daydreaming
Other similar activities	Other similar activities

Professor Ornstein also found that people who were trained to use one side of their brain more or less exclusively were relatively unable to use the other side. Even more significantly, he found that when the 'weaker' of the two brains was stimulated and encouraged to work in cooperation with the stronger side, it could do so, and the end result was a great increase in overall ability.

Thus it is unfortunate in some ways that Western education has traditionally been built upon 'the three Rs' – reading, writing and arithmetic – because these are all left-brain functions. We all know that many young children paint wonderfully imaginatively, but by the time they reach their teens this spontaneous creativity has somehow vanished.

Of course, much of our working lives – and certainly in the achievement of superefficiency – is dependent on the left brain. However, teaching ourselves to be more creative – or, more precisely, teaching ourselves to reactivate our lost creative faculties – will depend upon getting our sluggish right brains busy again. Happily Ornstein's findings prove that doing so will simultaneously stimulate our left brain, so that becoming more imaginative can only improve our total performance. (You may remember that in the Introduction it was baldly stated that many highly creative people are also highly organized; now you can see the justification for that view.)

Nor need you fear, as some people do, that your brain's capacity is limited, and that forcing it to do things it is not used to doing may in some way wear it out. The opposite is true. We use up only between 4 and 10 per cent of our brain cells throughout our lives, and leading brain researchers have proved in many studies that if we stimulate our brains they actively replenish themselves, increasing the number of interconnections by which they function.

It will be a long, long time – like forever – before computers can compete with that.

Stimulating Ideas

We'll soon be considering the best modern techniques for stimulating ideas. But before doing so it is important to note that the single most essential quality you need is confidence. Modesty and humility are charmingly winsome characteristics, but you won't find them in superabundance among creative people.

There are many explanations for this, some of which relate to inexcusable, and unpalatable, arrogant vanity. However, the excusable and reasonable reason for creative people's forceful bravura derives from their constant need to fight for their ideas. Although all modern organizations pretend, and even want, to welcome new ideas, they rarely do so. Creative people discover that fact quickly and painfully. That is why they develop – if they were not born with – sufficient self-assurance to rebuff criticism and fight for their ideas. Their confidence is their armour.

And the more confident they are, the more ideas they get; the less confident, the fewer. It will, you will find, be the same for you: if you lack the confidence, you won't have the ideas, so you won't gain the confidence . . . it is essential to break the circle, and only you can do it.

Now let us see how, with the problem analysed, we can generate some ideas that will solve it:

Imagination activation Think of a common, simple object – a paperclip, say – and then invent as many uses for it as you can in ten minutes. For a paperclip you might get:

Pipe cleaner	Fuse wire
Nail cleaner	Letter opener
Tie clip	Catapult missile
Ear de-waxer	Toothpick
Picture hook	Cufflink
Small hole poker	Ornament
Screwdriver	Typewriter cleaner
Fishing hook	Tension reducer
Broken bra strap mender	(like worry beads)
Zip fastener tag	

Doubtless you can think of more (and at different times

I've used paperclips for six of the above, so they are not wholly unrealistic).

This trains your mind to think imaginatively and is a good 'game' for two or three people. A fashionable variant, which is fun to play but not to be taken too seriously, is to invent unlikely new products for designer names. How about Gucci toilet paper or Pierre Cardin bicycle clips?

Bisociation   The great writer Arthur Koestler in his book *The Act of Creation*[15] describes the process of creativity as one of 'bisociation': putting together two unconnected facts or ideas to form a single idea. The best way to learn bisociative thinking is by making word chains. Open the dictionary and point to a word, any word. Then rapidly think of another word which is associated with it in your mind. Don't look for logical connections, but don't reject them if they occur naturally. You should be able to rush through at least fifty words in five minutes, then you'll need a short rest – it is surprisingly exhausting – before you start again.

How would someone else?   This technique is similar to the decision aid 'Ask the world's greatest authority' (Chapter 3), but it is employed here for a different purpose. When used as a decision aid it is simply intended to help you ensure you have seen the problem from all logical angles, which is why it refers to an 'authority'. To stimulate your imagination you should try to view the situation, like a novelist or playwright, through other people's eyes, conjecturing what they would feel and think and say. Often this will help you bisociate their 'thoughts' with your own, to create an utterly new perspective.

Think small   Many executives labour in vain to have big, earth-shattering (or at least organization-quaking) ideas and so fail to come up with the small but brilliant squibs by which most progress is made. You probably aren't Archimedes or Einstein or Newton or even Henry Ford, so you may never revolutionize mankind's beliefs, let alone the automobile industry. But if you could think of a way to simplify the sales order form your labour would not be in vain.

Lateral thinking The concept of lateral thinking, invented by Edward de Bono, relates closely to the left brain/right brain division described earlier. Lateral thinking consists of sideways leaps of the imagination (right brain activity), as contrasted with vertical thinking, the continuous progression down a logical chain of reasoning (left brain activity). De Bono sums up the differences as follows[16]:

Vertical thinking	*Lateral thinking*
Chooses	Changes
Looks for what is right	Looks for what is different
One thing must follow directly from another	Makes deliberate jumps
Concentrates on relevance	Welcomes chance intrusions
Moves in the most likely directions	Explores the least likely

In de Bono's words, you can stimulate lateral thinking if you 'arrange discontinuity', and the techniques he recommends for triggering off discontinuity include:

(a) free thinking, allowing your mind to wander over alternative and in many cases apparently irrelevant ways of looking at the situation
(b) deliberately exposing yourself to new influences in the form of people, articles, books, indeed, anything which might give you a different insight, even though it might not be immediately relevant
(c) switching from problem to problem
(d) using analogies to spark off ideas. The analogy should be suggested by the problem, but should then be allowed to exist in its own right to indicate a different way of looking at the problem

(e) arranging for the cross-fertilization of ideas with other people.

Edward de Bono's lateral thinking approach has been widely influential over recent years, perhaps because it adopts a simultaneous negative/positive technique to the stimulation of ideas: *stop* thinking vertically, *start* thinking laterally. It isn't always easy but if you can do it, it works.

Keep an ideas box   Leo Burnett, whose views on job obsession may not have been quite right, was none the less an advertising creative genius, and one of the ways he stimulated his own creativity was by keeping an ideas box. In it he stuffed, randomly, any article or picture or thought which struck him by its originality and which he guessed might some day prove useful. Whenever he was searching for a new advertising campaign he would rifle through his ideas box, and it usually helped. Other people in advertising look through books illustrating great campaigns of the past, not to copy them but to be stimulated.

Cliché killing   Apart from confidence, the most essential quality necessary for the self-stimulation of successful ideas is determination: resolute, firm determination.

Successful ideas are hard to come by. If they weren't this chapter would have been unnecessary and we would doubtless all be millionaires. (Having successful ideas won't *necessarily* make you rich, but it's an excellent starter.) The force which fights hardest against new ideas is mental fatigue: you have been trying to find a genuinely new solution for days or weeks, but the idea hasn't materialized, time is running out, and you will have to make do with a well-worn notion (which at least has proved itself before, you console yourself).

It's a hurdle we all fail to jump occasionally. Even the greatest writers, painters and composers sporadically produce work that is less than sparklingly original. All that can be said is that you must hold off the cliché solution to the very last. Those who take the easy option and accept the timeworn so they can go and have a drink (or turn to some simpler problem) soon lose the use of their right brain, which in my view shows they are not in their right mind.

KEY TIP Instead of counting sheep or reading yourself to sleep, allow your mind to meander casually over any knotty problem in need of solution, and there is a fair chance that an idea will emerge from your subconscious the next day.

Note that two key words are 'meander casually'; if you are the kind of person likely to worry yourself into a sweaty insomniac frenzy, then ignore the tip completely and move on quickly to a brainstorming session.

Brainstorming

Brainstorming sessions are defined by leading enthusiast J. Geoffrey Rawlinson as[17]: 'A means of getting a large number of ideas from a group of people in a short time.' Rawlinson himself claims to have generated over 1200 ideas for a chicken-food manufacturer in a three-and-threequarter-hour session, which my pocket calculator makes 5.3 ideas per minute, or one idea every 11.3 seconds for nearly four hours.

Rawlinson's awesome strike rate none the less ranks tardily behind the latest *Guinness Book of Records* attempt, in which ten British managers sprinted through 280 ideas for improving the British economy in just 480 seconds: that's one per 1.7 seconds. (They actually produced 464 ideas, but tossed out 184 of them for being too similar or too silly.)

Brainstorming sessions were invented by Alex F. Osborn in the 1930s, and popularized in the 1950s and '60s by Osborn[18] and Sidney J. Parnes[19], at which time they became highly fashionable. Later they fell into disuse, but in the 1980s they seem to be enjoying a swing-of-the-pendulum resurgence.

Osborn considered the following two principles indispensable to successful brainstorming:

> *Suspension of critical judgement.* People can think up more good ideas in a given length of time if they eliminate criticism and defer judgement until after the session
>
> *Quantity breeds quality.* The more ideas you have, the more likely you are to arrive at the best solution.

From these principles he developed the following rules for running brainstorming sessions:

Adverse criticism is taboo Ideas must be accepted, not judged, and participants must never be made to feel foolish (one of the greatest inhibitors of idea creation). Sarcastic laughter, raised eyebrows or shrugged shoulders are just as negative as outright criticism, and are similarly prohibited.

Free-wheeling is welcomed 'The wilder the idea, the better; it is easier to tame down than to think up' (Osborn in *Applied Imagination*[18]). This you will recognize as one of de Bono's principles of lateral thinking.

Combination and improvement are sought 'In addition to contributing ideas of their own, participants should suggest how the ideas of others can be turned into better ideas, or how two or more ideas can be joined into still another idea' (Osborn, *op. cit.*). This you will recognize as being similar to Koestler's concept of bisociation. You can now see that, although the techniques change, the basic principles of idea generation do not vary greatly.

No editorializing Ideas should not be elaborated or defended, just quickly stated and recorded.

Don't overlook the obvious The idea may not be obvious to everyone; it may well be possible to twist an obvious idea into something not so obvious; and anyway the obvious solution is sometimes the best.

Don't fear repetition It isn't worth worrying whether an idea has been suggested earlier, and jumping on someone for being repetitive is a type of criticism. Furthermore, ideas usually trigger different responses if repeated at different times during the session.

Quantity is the aim As has been stated, the more ideas generated, the greater the likelihood that one will be right.

Brainstorming sessions should comprise between four and twelve people, all of more or less equal status (if a big chief is present some people will inevitably be inhibited while others, equally inevitably, will show off).

Forty minutes is generally a good duration. If you continue for over an hour exhaustion usually sets in and it is better to close a session while enthusiasm is still unflagging. And you'll need either a tape recorder or an excellent secretary.

The group leader is obviously very important. The leader should be a born enthusiast, unselfish and friendly, a fast thinker, a good talker, with an instinct for audience reaction and a keen desire to see the session succeed. However, the role of the leader is not that of a meeting chairman; the leader merely gets things started with a simple statement of the problem – it must be a 'simple' problem, brainstorming sessions cannot cope with calculus – and steers the group in the right direction, praising ideas generously and encouraging other group members to build upon them.

Before leaving brainstorming, it must be mentioned that recent researches have suggested that individuals carrying out their own solitary sessions may generate more ideas than people brainstorming in groups. Studies have shown that four people working individually and combining their output often do better than four people brainstorming together. However, the matter is still open to debate and there is no doubt that for training purposes – to teach yourself the techniques of brainstorming – group participation is highly beneficial. Once you have seen how it is done you most certainly can, if you prefer, thereafter do your own thing.

Another, possibly more serious, disadvantage of group sessions stems from the problem of evaluating all the ideas. Think, for instance, of the ten British managers' 280 ideas for improving the economy. Even if it were possible to strike a red magic marker through half of them – and it doubtless was – that would still leave the other 50 per cent in need of further investigation.

That's 140 ideas, almost by definition impossible to rank for priority, and all of them bastards – that is, without a loving parent who feels responsible for them. We all know what becomes of ideas without parents, particularly ideas that are radically new and difficult to effect. They get lost in the filing system; they get left till the end of meetings and postponed; and postponed; and postponed again; until they pass forlorn and forgotten to the great idea graveyard in the sky.

This teaches us three things. First, evaluating ideas is as important as having them; second, ideas need to be nurtured and pushed vigorously forward; and, third, brainstorming sessions are a pathetic waste of time if the ideas generated are not taken under the wing of somebody with the determination, and the authority, to progress them.

Idea Evaluation

At a certain stage in its development the evaluation of an idea, certainly an idea of any magnitude, may well become a major project, involving many of the organization's departments and resources. Indeed, project evaluation is the subject of innumerable weighty management tomes. All that we can do here, then, is develop guidelines that will help you to differentiate between those ideas which should probably be stifled in their infancy and those ideas worth kicking on (remembering all the while that many of mankind's greatest inventions seemed utterly looney to begin with).

There are six questions to ask of any new idea:

Is it really new?
Is it both relevant and practical?
Who will it involve?
How much will it cost?
How much will it save?
Will it require more formal evaluation?

Is it really new? You may genuinely believe your idea to be new, but you may be wrong. Try hard to discover the truth. If the idea has already been used elsewhere and failed, this will emerge at some stage and you will by then (a) have wasted a lot of time and (b) have egg on your face.

Is it both relevant and practical? At the start of this chapter we mentioned those people who sparkle with ideas which never happen. That's because most of their ideas are either irrelevant or impractical. Admittedly it is sometimes far from easy to tell whether an infant idea is or is not practical – who would have dreamed huge metallic objects could fly? But that is no excuse for not attempting to assess the practicality of any idea; at least you will then be aware of the difficulties in store. (And if you have carried out the problem analysis correctly, *your* ideas should always be relevant.)

Who will it involve? More crucially, who will it upset? It is unusual, not to say unknown, for a new idea not to upset someone, if not everyone. Unless you identify who and why in advance they will hear a garbled version of the idea on the grapevine and do their darndest to demolish it.

How much will it cost? It is unusual, not to say unknown, for new ideas not to cost a penny, and you can be certain it will be the first question your boss raises. If you don't have the answer you'll look daft, as many executives regularly do.

How much will it save? This is often much harder to calculate, but it is always worth making a guestimate. If you cannot perceive any financial saving whatsoever, it may not be as good an idea as you thought.

Will it require more formal evaluation? Obviously most of the above questions relate principally to comparatively small projects. If the idea you are proposing is a submarine-cum-aeroplane which can travel both under-water and in the air, you are unlikely to be able to say how much it will cost or save, or who it will involve, just like that. But if further, formal evaluation is required, costs will be incurred, and they will need to be assessed and justified in advance.

Now you've had the idea and asked the six questions, and you still want to press ahead. What next?

Winning Through

In many ways having an idea is child's play compared with getting something done about it. As has already been remarked, people and organizations obstinately insist that they welcome ideas enthusiastically and equally obstinately reject them.

Nevertheless, a few ideas do eventually win through despite the odds, opposition and unpopularity. And to help you ensure that yours are among the winners here are idea-nurturing tactics:

Don't think people think the way you think Ideas, in their infancy, are often vague and wispy things. So when you describe them, other people may well misunderstand you. Take great care to communicate your idea in their language. (Remember Chapter 1: messages that are not encoded clearly clearly cannot be decoded.)

Decide whether you want to get the credit or to get the idea accepted The two are frequently mutually exclusive. Sometimes you may get action on an idea. Sometimes you may get the credit for it. Seldom can you get both. Decide which you want.

Arrange for someone else to have your idea A corollary of the previous tactic. Suggest the idea, by inference and innuendo, to the most powerful person in the group you are trying to influence. Once he has been persuaded that it was his own idea, allow him to win you round to it, step by step. This will (a) get your idea through and (b) convince him that you are an extremely reasonable person who can recognize a good idea even when it is someone else's.

Be casual Clinical detachment is a great help. You are, quite rightly, passionately and obsessively committed to your idea, but it is almost always a bad idea to show it.

Employ decoys Put up a decoy idea first. Allow it to be shot down, but only after fierce argument. Then put up the real idea, which will probably be allowed to fly because (a) your colleagues now feel a little guilty about killing your first idea and/or (b) they are probably now exhausted.

Don't overstress originality The more original your idea, the less you should stress the fact. Mention similar-sounding ideas that have been successful. This will greatly reassure those who find all true innovation disconcerting.

Add warm, emotional appeal If you can encourage some well-hated person in the organization to oppose your idea, you will be virtually guaranteed of success. Alternatively, you may be able to achieve the same effect by mentioning the likelihood of the organization's most hated competitor getting in first.

Just occasionally people have brilliantly simple ideas which they keep to themselves because they fear somebody will say: 'That's so obvious, why didn't you think of it before?'

Never let such worries enter your head: if you've a good idea, promulgate it. Many of the best ideas are indeed absurdly obvious – after someone has had them.

Should anyone be so foolish as to make the above remark, the following semi-rhetorical question should squash them: 'It would never have struck me as sensible to blame Newton for not having discovered gravity when he was younger – but presumably you think otherwise?'

6

TO TRAVEL CREATIVELY

If your work does not involve much glamorous globe-trotting it may seem odd that creative travelling is one of the keys to superefficiency. Yet a study published in *IBM Systems Journal*[20] showed that 13.1 per cent of top management's time and 6.4 per cent of *all* executives' time is spent travelling.

Moreover, those percentages relate to working time: they do not include time spent travelling to and from work. If you commute for only an hour a day, thirty minutes each way, that will account for approximately 10 per cent of your working week, and the figure could well be doubled if you live and work in one of the major conurbations.

So even if you don't spend your time flitting twixt Rome and Reykjavik and Rio de Janeiro, you probably spend at least 250 hours each year – that's about thirty full working days – traipsing between home and office. And it is all but inconceivable that you couldn't use that time more creatively than you do. So, before flying up and away, let us consider our more mundane daily odysseys between domicile and desk.

Commuting

Most books on the subject start by recommending that you avoid wasting time commuting by living as close to your work as possible. In today's world that advice seems about as helpful as the ancient Irish joke about the way to Killarney: (Q: 'What's the best way from here to Killarney?' A: 'If it's the best way to Killarney you're looking for, you shouldn't be starting from here in the first place.')

Where you choose to live is always one of the most carefully considered of decisions, dependent on a host of factors from cost to children's education (and an ideal subject for a thorough Ben Franklin decision analysis when next you are thinking of moving). If you live somewhere that is inconvenient for your work then the likelihood, verging on the certainty, is that you have chosen to live there for a variety of reasons and intend to stay there, at least for now.

Commuting time need not be wasted time. Free from personal and telephonic interruptions – though modern telephone systems are changing that – the hours you spend commuting, whether by train, car or local transport, can be the most productive and creative of the day. But since it is all too easy to fritter away commuting time in a vacuous trance, it is essential to begin by detailing some of the things to be avoided, the 'Don'ts', before aiming at the 'Dos'.

'DON'TS'

Don't play the radio If you commute by car, don't switch on the radio for background buzz; if you are not consciously listening, switch off. It is impossible to think clearly with someone prattling away in your car.

Don't lane hop When you reach the inevitable traffic jam, don't lane hop. 'The other lane moves faster' is one of Murphy's Laws you should disobey. If you attempt to lane hop while thinking about other things your car will end up with rounded corners, your no-claims policy will end up in the bin, and you will end up at work suffering from frayed nerves, mental exhaustion and hooting in the ears.

Don't set off at the last minute   Leave an extra seven minutes for someone else's breakdown. It will mean you generally arrive at work seven minutes early, which is hardly catastrophic, but it will also mean that if a car ahead of you breaks down or has a small shunt in a traffic jam, you won't sit in your car fuming and frenzied by the delay. (Even if the stoppage delays you ten or twelve minutes you will still be only a little late.) If your own car breaks down or if there is a major accident, there is little that you can do except accept the cruelty of fate.

Don't hold commuters' parties   If you commute by train, don't become matey with the other passengers. If this sounds unfriendly that's because it is unfriendly. Once you become chummy with the other passengers you will end up playing bridge, drinking in the bar, criticizing television, the government, teenagers and your local soccer team – but you will never again get much work done. If you commute by train for year after year and meet the same folk in the same carriage day after day, it takes an iron will to remain as silent as a Trappist monk, but it will prove worth it.

Don't read newspapers   That may seem to be ostrich-like philistinism, but once you open the paper you will spend the entire journey reading it, and poring over the paper from cover to cover is a leisure activity, not an essential. Superefficiency is, in large measure, about setting priorities. In an era of excellent television and radio news, reading daily newspapers is not – unless you are a politician – a priority. Skip-read the headlines, key items and material relevant to your industry either before you leave home or over coffee at work. Catch up with the important news via the serious Sundays. Sadly, if you wish to use your commuting time efficiently the same goes for novels.

Having listed the habits to be avoided, let's now consider the ways to use commuting usefully, whether you do so by train or car.

CAR 'DOS'

Set yourself problems Far and away the most effective and most enjoyable way to spend driving time is to set yourself a tricky problem at the start of the journey which you *must* solve by the finish. Obviously you can only set, and solve, problems requiring no writing or difficult calculation – creative and personnel problems, simple reorganizations, sales promotions and the like are all ideal. Scribbling notes at 70 m.p.h. on the motorway is not to be recommended, so you will probably find it helpful to keep a small dictating machine to hand. And setting yourself problems makes driving time pass quickly as well as productively.

Concentrating on problems is, for some reason, far easier in cars than on trains; perhaps this is because one almost always sits opposite people on trains, and it is embarrassingly difficult to know where to stare while concentrating. (Maybe the answer is to close your eyes; but then there is a fair chance – particularly in the evening – that you'll fall asleep and miss your stop!)

Carry a colleague If you live near one of your work colleagues, arrange to drive in together from time to time when you have a mutual problem to discuss or when one of you wants information from the other. Such private chats are often far more honest and fruitful than conversations of similar duration at work.

It is better for such joint journeyings not to become daily routine. Make clear that you are not being unsociable: you usually prefer to commute alone but greatly appreciate the opportunity for a conversation when there is something on your mutual agenda.

Go on a cassette course Do you want to learn a language or more about salesmanship or accountancy or computers? There are many training courses available on cassettes, and commuting is a perfect time for them.

Rehearse, rehearse Another advantage of cars over trains is that you can talk to yourself aloud without anyone thinking it odd. You can rehearse presentations and speeches, timing them against the car clock, until you become word perfect. There is nobody to hear you, mistakes don't matter; indeed, short of hiring a rehearsal room, there are few better occasions for the purpose. (Though I advocate it, and do it, I still find rehearsing to myself aloud in my office embarrassing.)

Dictation time In addition to using a dictating machine to remind yourself of thoughts and ideas (see 'Set yourself problems', page 123) a further advantage of being able to talk aloud is that you can dictate letters and documents for your secretary to type later.

Telephone time Car telephones have proved far less useful than expected by many of the executives who have acquired them. They are indubitably handy for letting people know you are jammed in a jam and will be late. But for a host of reasons they are not much use for general business conversations: you tend to be driving during non-working hours; you cannot coordinate them with paperwork; it is difficult to deal with many types of query; and so on. Having said that, car telephones are highly useful to those in jobs calling for endless driving, such as sales management and retail coordination.

TRAIN 'DOS'

Writing time The overriding advantage that trains (and planes) offer over driving is the facility for writing. Many great writers, including John Le Carré, have written entire books on trains so it should be perfectly possible for you to pen proposals and projects in transit. The following hints will facilitate the process:

Surprising though it seems, it is best *not* to sit at a table; train seats and tables do not move together in harmony, which makes writing exceedingly difficult. Instead you must carry your own table – a firm, flat, smooth briefcase – to rest on your knees.

Inside the briefcase you will obviously need writing equipment and relevant documents; plus a small stapling machine (this is one use for which paperclips are not suitable – they catch themselves into too many papers); plus a pocket calculator; plus rubbers and a pencil sharpener if you use pencils – advisable on a train, because the jogging inevitably causes occasional illegibility; plus scissors if you are one of those writers who likes to cut up documents and reposition paragraphs.

Choose a seat from which your writing elbow pokes into a gangway, rather than into the passenger sitting next to you.

Avoid writing documents for which you need to keep referring to lots of source material, since even if you are able to carry the material with you you will find it slow and awkward to consult.

Do not try to write highly confidential documents unless you are sure the train will be empty: the sniff of a whiff of confidentiality will guarantee that your neighbours keep trying to peek.

Reading time Reading, like writing, is one of the obvious advantages of trains over cars. Depending upon whether you are a lark or an owl, you will find it better to read complex reports in the morning/evening and trade magazines and direct-mail shots in the evening/morning.

Discussion time If you are taking a lengthy (probably non-commuter) journey with colleagues, consider reserving an entire compartment so that you can talk openly. British Rail will not issue seat reservations without tickets, so you may need to buy and waste a couple of tickets. That could be a small price to pay for the working hours gained. (Moreover, if you want to behave naughtily you can probably get a refund on the unused tickets afterwards. Ssshh . . .)

Brainstorming time Finally, while it has been pointed out above that trains are not quite as suitable as cars for solitary concentration, they are excellent for solitary brainstorming sessions in which you sit with pad and pen and note down ideas as you brainstorm them. After maybe half an hour, when you've generated thirty or forty ideas (318 if you can equal J. Geoffrey Rawlinson's strike rate), you can use the remainder of the journey for an initial evaluation, so that by the time the journey is over you will be down to half a dozen ideas worth taking further.

Tips for Trips

The essence of commuting is that it is repetitive; business trips, in contrast, tend to be varied, even if you make some of them regularly. When commuting you can plan for the predictable, whereas on trips you must plan for the unpredictable. (All travel involves bungles, breakdowns and delays, but when you are commuting the scope for disasters, though considerable, is limited; on trips it is unlimited.)

The first vital step is, therefore, to find a good travel agent. The concept of a *perfect* travel agent is probably a contradiction in terms, but some are a great deal better than most, and a lousy travel agent will enthusiastically seize all the unlimited opportunities available to botch up your trip.

As with accountants and solicitors, when searching for a good travel agent the firm is far less important than the individual you deal with, and the only way to discover such people is by personal recommendation or painful trial and error. If your organization has a travel department, then, of course, your hands are tied and you will be forced to use the system.

> **KEY TIP** To obtain an initial indication of a travel agent's competence, ask him to sort out an almost impossible trip – for example, you need to be in Bombay for dinner (restaurant to be recommended, please), leaving Heathrow not earlier than 9 p.m. the night before and stopping in Nairobi for a meeting en route. The intelligence and enthusiasm with which the task is tackled will reveal a great deal.

Having found your agent – and if your first choice makes a hash of it change immediately; agents who goof on your first trip can be absolutely relied upon to goof again and again – you are ready to plan your journey. Check your passport; check whether a visa and/or health precautions are required; choose comfortable, loose clothes for the flight, and then follow these thirteen lucky tips which will help to smooth your trip.

Build in bungle margins This is particularly crucial in winter, when schedules regularly go awry. The temptation to fix meetings within an hour of the flight's scheduled landing is often great, but to be resisted if humanly possible. An extra hour's grace will enable you to freshen up and relax – or to be on time if the flight isn't.

Prepare outline alternatives The chairman of one of the country's leading companies used to have hotel rooms booked for him in every major town on his flight route, in case of a forced landing. That's a trifle extravagant, but it is worth getting your travel agent to provide alternative flight times and routes, and to check the probability of weather problems at your destination. (Milan, for example, is frequently fogged in after dusk in late autumn, but few agents bother to mention it.) If problems seem likely, book an extra night at your hotel; it can easily be cancelled.

Travel light Most trippers take far too many items of

clothing and return with half of them unworn. This is troublesome, a quick way to a hernia, and the more you pack the more creased everything will get. (N.B. Hanging garments out in a steamy bathroom helps creases fall out quickly.)

Keep a trip list If you travel frequently, establish a checklist of things you always need to take and to do, to which you can refer before each journey.

Avoid rush hours If you cannot avoid them, allow for them. The time taken to travel to and from the airport of any major city in the world will be at least doubled between 7.30 and 10.00 a.m. and between 4.30 and 7.00 p.m. local time.

Check time shifts Everybody gets time changes wrong occasionally, but that is no excuse, and no help when it happens. It is always worth double-checking.

Take small change It is embarrassing and unnecessary to find yourself with only travellers' cheques or large-denomination notes when leaving your first taxi or tipping the porter. Get the bank, or whoever, to include some small change among your currency. If you travel a fair amount, after each trip store the change you have obtained for the next trip, using a separate envelope for each currency. Then remember to take the envelope on your next visit to that country!

Carry a useful numbers list To avoid struggling with local operators and directories, before you leave prepare a list of the local addresses and telephone numbers you are likely to need; and carry, separately, a list of your credit card numbers in case of mishap.

Take your time International travel will soon wear you to a frazzle if you cut everything fine, arriving at the airport in the nick of time, rushing through check-in, pushing your way first off the plane and jumping queues for taxis. There will, unavoidably, be occasions when you cannot avoid rushing and scurrying, but if you do it perpetually neither your fellow passengers nor your blood pressure will thank you.

Carry a portable office   Flights and hotel rooms provide even better opportunities for solitary and uninterrupted concentration than trains and cars. Make sure you carry the wherewithal to be able to work wherever you are (the list is the same as for trains).

Keep in touch   Tempting though it may be to behave like a free-wheeling roving reporter once you land on foreign soil, it will drive everyone else bananas. Ensure your secretary or somebody at the office has a written itinerary, and telephone back to base regularly. When phoning, dictate to your secretary notes to yourself, and follow them up on your return.

Make friends with the concierge   In most foreign hotels the concierge is a person of considerable power and influence, capable of booking you into full restaurants, obtaining tickets for sold-out shows, amending your travel arrangements and getting taxis in the pouring rain. He is worth befriending immediately on arrival; a little instant financial lubrication will not go amiss.

Check feast days and strikes   You might imagine that efficient travel agents would forewarn you of foreign feast days and holidays, but they rarely do, particularly if the holiday comes in the middle of a three- or four-day trip. Either get an international calendar with such days marked or remember to ask beforehand. Local strikes are more difficult to keep track of, but they interfere with a traveller's life surprisingly often, and it is well worth checking whether any are in progress before you leave.

These thirteen lucky tips will help you skip numbly over most tripwires. However, there are two other subjects which must also be considered: what useful items should you take with you, and how should you cope on your return?

All experienced travellers accumulate an idiosyncratic collection of mascot-like items without which they never like to set forth. They might always carry a corkscrew or a Swiss penknife, a whistle with which to call taxis, or – as one woman traveller recommends – photographs of spouse and infants with which to dampen the ardour of lecherous males. The following half-dozen are more commonplace and all worth considering:

Multi-socket adaptor   Mini sewing kit
Travelling iron   Analgesics and antacids
Dry-cleaning spray   Sellotape, in dispenser

Second, how should you cope on your return? If you have been absent for long a mountainous pile of paper will be stacked high in your in-tray; and in addition you will rapidly need to progress the work resulting from your trip.

With regard to your in-tray, get your secretary or an assistant to divide all incoming material into three categories:

Urgent documents and queries
Non-urgent documents
Magazines and bumph.

If you will be going home before going into work, have the urgent documents and queries sent there ahead of you, so you can quickly rifle through them before you re-enter your organization's portals; alternatively, get to work an hour early so you can do the same thing. If you are going straight back to work, try to creep in unnoticed so you can brief yourself before the hubbub begins.

Nor should you leave the non-urgent documents too long, as your secretary may mistakenly have miscategorized something demanding instant attention. But once you have satisfied yourself that the non-urgent documents are indeed non-urgent, put them aside, to be read during the next seventy-two hours. And deal with the magazines and bumph as and when you can.

You should put in hand any work arising from your trip within twenty-four hours; if you leave it longer it will slip away dangerously. Remember to write letters thanking people who have been especially helpful or hospitable; and remember to make notes, for yourself, of people who haven't and of things that went wrong.

Finally, no trip that lasts more than forty-eight hours should be all work and no play. If you are away for several days you should manage to squeeze in at least a few hours' relaxation.

Find out which are the best eateries and entertainments before you go in case you are left to your own devices; take your international driving licence in case you want to hire a car; if you are going somewhere warm, remember your swimming gear; get a phrase book, as you may well wish to wander off the tourist track; and don't forget to consult the concierge.

KEY TIP If you've time for sightseeing but dislike packaged coach tours, pick up a coach-tour leaflet, decide which of the sights appeals to you, and plan your own personal tour in a taxi or on foot.

Jet Lag

Jet lag is probably the only one of mankind's ailments which could not have existed before the middle of the twentieth century and which has been created by mankind itself. Fortunately, though disagreeable, it is not too lethal a malady.

Jet lag is principally caused by the disruptions to your underlying biological and body temperature rhythms which result from changing time zones. However, researchers specializing in the subject have shown that other factors also contribute to its effects, particularly:

The stress and fatigue of flying
The excitement and apprehension associated with the
    purpose of the trip
Non-rhythmical aspects of the unfamiliar environment
    – diet, climate, social customs and the rest.

All these combine with the time change to create feelings of exhaustion and listlessness and to impair concentration. It has been shown that on average it takes one day to recover fully from one hour's time change – i.e. about six days for six hours – and that it takes somewhat longer after an eastward flight than after a westward flight.

You cannot completely escape the effects of jet lag, but you can minimize the damage in three ways:

1 Adjust your sleeping schedule by a couple of hours in the days prior to departure
2 Ensure that you have one full day of inactivity after arrival
3 Thereafter enter wholeheartedly into the social activities and local time schedules; the evidence shows that the more you ignore jet lag, the quicker it goes away.

Lastly, when you know you will be suffering from jet lag make sure you book into a hotel with a TV set in the room and twenty-four-hour service (which by no means includes all the most expensive luxury establishments). You are likely both to want a sandwich in the middle of the night and to doze in front of the TV in the afternoon, and it is nicer if there is no problem about either.

Holidays

The possibility of devoting a few hours of your holiday to reading general-interest, and hopefully self-improving, business books has already been mentioned (Chapter 2).

This section is about preparing for your holidays and coping with other people's.

It is in your own selfish interest to prepare for your holiday superefficiently. If things go wrong because you failed to tie up the loose ends before leaving, this will (a) not endear you to your bosses and colleagues and (b) face you with a ghastly mess on your return.

To minimize the risk of such occurrences you should carry out the following five-point plan:

Make your main holiday a spring-cleaning time Make a special effort to complete as many jobs as possible before you go and avoid, covertly if needs be, undertaking new tasks in the week before your departure.

Prepare an 'in progress' schedule Draft a detailed report covering the status of all projects, noting who is doing what and what should be done by when, and distribute it to all concerned.

Send a 'possible problems' memo This should go to your boss, confidentially, warning him of likely spanners in the works, with recommendations on how to deal with them.

Speak to all and sundry Telephone or meet every possible spanner-thrower in the forty-eight hours before departing, to confirm they know exactly what they should be doing in your absence, and that they foresee no problems you have not foreseen.

Hang around a little Do not, as most people do, scuttle off early the day before your holiday, but stay a bit later than usual to check everything is in order and to allow last-minute problems to raise their inconvenient heads.

Having taken these precautions, whether or not you leave a contact address or telephone number is entirely up to you. Many executives hate the notion of their holidays being interrupted; others can only relax serenely if they know dreadful disasters will be communicated to them instead of being allowed to fester. It's a matter of personal taste.

When it is your colleagues' turn to go on holiday you should aim to convince them that it is likewise in their interest to implement the five-point plan. At first sight it might seem marvellously Machiavellian – especially when you are not greatly enamoured of the colleagues concerned – to allow them to botch their departure if they know no better. But such schemes have a nasty habit of rebounding, and you may well find yourself spending their holiday sorting out their problems because they have not done so first.

Incidentally, when secretaries go on holiday and temps take over, make a great deal of fuss beforehand to ensure that the temp you get is intelligent and competent; unintelligent, incompetent temps can upset customers, confuse colleagues and cause chaos unlimited. Get them in for a day before they are needed, so they are fully briefed and know where everything is when they arrive to start work. (Otherwise they will spend the first two days asking *you* where everything is – and you haven't the foggiest notion, have you?)

Some executives prefer to go on holiday at the same time as their secretaries, arguing that otherwise their secretaries do little or nothing for three or four weeks each year while their own efficiency is impaired by having to use temps. Quite apart from the silly gossip this practice invariably provokes, it is always a bad idea. Both executive and secretary are employed by the organization, not by each other; and it is in the organization's interest for somebody who knows what is going on to be available at all times. Those who have spent days unravelling muddles when an executive and his secretary have vamoosed simultaneously will agree vigorously.

So as long as you've left your secretary behind and implemented your five-point plan, off you go – and have a good vacation. (Are you sure you don't want to leave your phone number?)

7

PEOPLE MANAGEMENT

Having reached the seventh and last key to superefficiency the wheel has turned full circle. 'The more efficiently you can cope with other people, the more efficient
you will be' stressed the introduction to the first key,
persuasive communication, quoting the poet John Donne's celebrated dictum, 'No man is an island.'

Now we return to this crucial subject. The initial
chapter, in a way, cheated. It concentrated on answering
the 'how to' questions – how to communicate, how to
write documents, how to make presentations – taking for
granted the more fundamental questions: what should be
communicated, when and why? Yet unless you answer
these questions correctly you might merely become more
adept at communicating the wrong things at the wrong
times for the wrong reasons, which would hardly be a
superefficient recipe for success.

Ultimately, all the principles of management are guidelines for the handling of people: how to motivate them,
how to organize them, how to delegate to them, how to
improve them, how to lead them.

There are no simple solutions. Human beings being
what they are – ambitious, touchy, self-centred, insecure
and frequently stroppy – and even more importantly what
they are not – unfailingly courteous, cheerful, diligent,

honest and truthful – nobody will ever succeed in man-ipulating them unerringly. (All the great leaders in history have fluffed some, if not many, of their personal rela-tionships.)

On the other hand, most of us are exceedingly good at handling most people most of the time. Except when emergencies and arguments arise, we cope successfully with colleagues and customers, shop assistants and sales-men, family and friends without even thinking about it.

So, once again, as with decision-making and many other aspects of superefficiency, the differences between those who are good at handling people and those who are not so good are differences of degree, not of kind. All of us are reasonably good at it, none of us is perfect, but some of us are far better than others. So you probably do not need to go on a lengthy and expensive course of psychotherapy in order to improve your handling of people; you merely need to stop doing the things you do badly, and do the things you do well a little better, neither of which should be beyond anyone's powers.

Let us, then, return to the five principles of people management – motivation, organization, delegation, im-provement and leadership – and (keeping in mind that they all overlap) consider each in turn.

MOTIVATION

Psychologists have defined mankind's motivations for working in different ways, but the most widely accepted analysis is that of Abraham Maslow[21]. He postulated the following hierarchy of motivations (running from bottom to top):

Self-fulfilment (achievements)
Self-esteem (status)
Social needs (acceptance)
Safety needs (protection from danger)
Physiological needs (hunger, thirst, sleep).

When a lower need has been satisfied, Maslow contends,

the next need in the hierarchy is aroused. Thus people who are hungry, thirsty, cold or afraid are not greatly concerned about self-fulfilment and self-esteem, a fact which has been confirmed by numerous psychological studies apart from Maslow's.

Establishing that the same applies to the upper levels of the hierarchy, where most executives operate, has proved less easy. It has certainly been shown that higher-level managers attach extra importance to autonomy and self-fulfilment, but the findings raise the inevitable chicken-and-egg problem: is it managers who get to the top who seek self-fulfilment or vice-versa?

Fortunately, from our parochial point of view, this academic dispute is, well, academic. The crucial, rarely disputed fact is that executives are motivated primarily by self-fulfilment and self-esteem, and secondarily by social acceptance. If you keep that in mind, then most of the following guidelines will fall logically into place.

Motivation is a forward-looking process. The degree to which any of us is motivated to carry out a task depends upon the perception that carrying out the task will help us achieve the results we desire. It follows from this that the common-sense proposition – people are motivated to carry out actions that will lead them towards things they want (and to avoid things they don't want) – is dependent upon rewards (and punishments). (Or, as researchers specializing in the psychology of donkeys will doubtless one day prove, upon carrots and sticks.)

To bring all this down to office level, in order to motivate those you work with successfully you continuously need to encourage them, not with promises of financial reward but by helping them enhance their self-esteem and self-fulfilment. (Of course, financial reward has a vital role to play in bolstering self-esteem; but for most people the money is a means not an end, which is why the vast majority of very rich people continue to work even though it is financially unnecessary for them to do so.)

Equally importantly, you must establish that the rewards are directly related to people's efforts. They must perceive this for themselves and know that you perceive it too. This is the foundation of Management By Objectives (MBO): if employees' work objectives are clearly defined and stated, they can attain self-fulfilment and self-esteem by achieving those objectives, boosted by the knowledge that their superiors and colleagues, too, will be aware of their achievement.

Much of this motivation (particularly discussions concerning MBO) can, and should, only be communicated infrequently – at annual salary reviews or appraisal time. It is impossible and unwise to draw attention incessantly to whether people are or are not achieving their longer-term goals. One of the prime purposes of MBO is to encourage people to encourage themselves: *self*-fulfilment and *self*-esteem.

However, motivation is an everyday business: you cannot motivate people – though many executives try – by encouraging them on the day of their annual appraisal and avoiding all personal involvement on the other 364 days. So here are five tips to help you motivate all around you all around the year:

Praise the praiseworthy Maybe it is traditional British detachment (Americans don't seem to suffer from the same difficulty) but many executives find it embarrassing to pay compliments when work is well done, particularly if it isn't quite perfect. If you suffer from this malaise you must cure it: return to the rules of persuasive communication, decide what you are going to say in advance, rehearse if necessary, and then force yourself to speak, smiling as you do so (the smile will disguise your embarrassment). You'll soon find it's as easy as falling off a swivel-and-tilt chair.

But don't overdo it If you gush too much and praise people too often or too easily, you will depreciate the value of the praise; occasionally, enthusiastically and sincerely should be the rule, not incessantly. glibly and unconvincingly.

Search for the praiseworthy As Blanchard and Johnson put it in *The One Minute Manager*[11]: 'Catch them doing something right.' If you indirectly hear about some laudable achievement, grab the opportunity to compliment the person responsible. Applause is still sweeter when it comes as a surprise.

Reprimand rapidly When a reprimand must be administered it is vital that it be done quickly; reprimands are as intrinsic to effective motivation as praise, provided they are accepted and understood by the person concerned, which is another reason why it is so crucial not to delay them (see Chapter 3, and stop procrastinating!).

Be specific Whether praising or blaming, be specific: don't discuss general attitudes and aptitudes – that's for appraisal time – but concentrate on the particular event concerned, and let the doer know why you, and the organization, view it with pleasure/displeasure.

Lastly, if you are responsible for a department or even a small group of people, have regular free-for-all meetings at which you encourage everyone to be utterly frank and open. Initially they won't be, but after a few sessions they'll gain confidence; and if they do not speak candidly on these occasions they will have poor grounds for grumbling behind your back. A working lunch with sandwiches is a good format, and monthly is a good frequency; but certainly such sessions should not be held more often, otherwise the occasions will be trivialized and degenerate into gossip parties.

KEY TIP The best motivator of all is to make work fun, so never be too stuffy to joke with all and sundry (but *counterfeit* jocularity is profoundly embarrassing and to be avoided like a dud cheque).

ORGANIZATION

Organization, like data processing and computer technology, is now a highly specialized subject and few executives get the opportunity to mastermind a major structural reorganization. None the less, most executives have to organize, or reorganize, small groups from time to time and it is then vital to know the principles involved.

First and most important, no organizational structure will work well without the willing participation of the senior managers. ('Senior' is here a comparative term: in a small department the senior managers may be quite junior.)

Note the word 'willing'. It is halfway between enthusiastic and antagonistic. Once upon a time it was believed that organizational structures could be foisted upon people with or without their consent. Some autocratic companies still act that way. It is a sure way to lose good people. Only those who cannot find other employment will knuckle under and accept reorganizations they dislike.

On the other hand, it is rare for people who are being reorganized to greet the new order enthusiastically (unless they themselves are being promoted as a result). As has been stressed before, most people are wary of most changes in their lives.

So your job, as organizer, is to gain their willing consent but not to be too optimistic of much more. To gain their willing consent you must present your plan persuasively, using all the skills of presentation and salesmanship that you possess (and that you picked up in Chapter 1). Any lesser attempt to carry the key people with you will end in at least temporary, and possibly permanent, hostility and inefficiency.

The second important fact about organizational structures, well known to all management consultants, is that they work on two levels: the formal and the informal.

The formal is the official structure as defined on paper, complete with job titles, little boxes and dotted lines. The informal is the matrix of interpersonal relationships which make it work. If two executives abominate each other's entrails they will not work together constructively no matter how many lines you draw between their boxes. Successful organizations work on both formal and informal levels; no organization can work well on either one without the other.

The third important fact about organizational structures is that there is no such thing as the perfect organizational structure. That is why, apparently inexplicably, management consultants will sometimes centralize, decentralize and then recentralize a company over the years. Sceptical outsiders suspect the mutations are merely designed to keep the management consultants in business. A more charitable, and realistic, explanation is that most companies and institutions need to be picked up and thoroughly shaken from time to time, and oscillatory reorganizations catalyse the process. The structure, whether centralized or decentralized, matters less than the hard thinking which such transformations enforce.

So it is well worth reviewing the structure of any department for which you are responsible, even if it appears to be working well, every couple of years. Don't just change for the sake of change; but make very sure you are not resisting change simply because of the headaches and opposition it will generate.

When you do carry out a structural reorganization here are three principles to keep in mind:

One boss per person Except for 'dotted-line' functional responsibilities – for example, to the buying department or finance department – it is always better for an individual to report to one boss only. This avoids conflicting orders, conflicting demands upon the individual's time, conflicting loyalties – and thence conflicts between the individual's several bosses.

The fewer levels the better Too many levels of hierarchy inhibit communication, minimize job satisfaction and create unnecessary work; flatter is better than deeper.

Avoid detailed job descriptions   In theory precisely specified job descriptions help executives know precisely
and specifically what their jobs entail; in practice they
create blinkered thinking and demarcation disputes. If
they are absolutely essential, keep them brief, as open as
possible, and relate them to objectives rather than activities.

Although organizational charts have been mentioned in
passing, they too, like job descriptions, are to be avoided
whenever possible. They make people exceedingly conscious of their superiority or inferiority; they make it
harder to change things in future; and they freeze personal relationships. As Robert Townsend, of *Up the
Organization*[22] fame, states: 'Never formalize, print and
circulate them. Good organizations are living bodies that
grow new muscles to meet challenges.'

DELEGATION

Delegation is one of the most difficult management arts.
The two main difficulties involve getting the balances
right – between delegating too much or too little, and
between over- or under-supervision. However, it is trans-
parently clear that you yourself can never succeed unless
you learn to delegate successfully. If you continue to carry
out too many routine chores you will never find time for
planning, for creativity, for building the business. You
will most certainly not be, or be seen to be, superefficient.
    Many management theorists confuse and cloud the
subject but there are really only three types of delegation:

Routine job delegation   This comprises jobs that could,
and doubtless one day will, be done by computers but are
now still done by people; jobs that require little (or often
definitely *nil*) creativity or imagination; jobs that can be
carried out by rote.

Specialist job delegation   This comprises jobs that can,
and should, be done by specialists – accountancy or law or

design. This is a comparatively easy type of delegation to handle, but many executives none the less botch it by behaving as if they are Renaissance men capable, like Leonardo da Vinci, of doing everything themselves. Specialists are not always right, but if they are any good at all they are always worth listening to. As modern life grows increasingly complex, successful top managers are using specialist consultants and advisers increasingly.

KEY TIP **Seek specialist advice whenever possible and reject two thirds of it.**

Training job delegation This is the most difficult, but in many ways the most important, type of delegation. It comprises jobs which will challenge and train your subordinates, jobs which call for thought and creativity, jobs which you might well have carried out yourself, and in which you will need to get personally involved again at a later stage. These are the delegated jobs which, properly handled, will motivate, encourage and fulfil those who work for you (they feel no more enthusiastic about the routine jobs than you used to feel yourself).

Concentrating principally on this third type of delegation (but the rules apply broadly to all three types), you must ensure when you delegate any major task that those concerned understand the following nine points:

Why the work needs to be done
What they are expected to do
The date by which it must be completed
The authority they have to make decisions
The problems that must be referred back to you
The progress reports, if any, that should be produced
The resources and help available to get the work done
The budget available, if relevant
The precise form of the final report or recommendation
   to be submitted.

Once you have thoroughly gone through these nine points let your subordinates get on with the job and leave them alone. If you meet in the corridor, ask cheerfully (but rhetorically), 'How is —— going?' Let them know that your door is always open if they get hopelessly stuck. But on no account pester them incessantly for hour-by-hour progress reports or they will feel you lack confidence in them and lose their enthusiasm and heart. Anyway, if you intended to take so close an interest in the job, why on earth didn't you do it yourself?

Never assume, however, unless you know the subordinate exceedingly well and therefore have supreme confidence, that the recommendation will be correct. Allocate a time when you can both go through the work together. (Never ever file away subordinates' recommendations without responding to them: it is deeply demoralizing, lousy management – and it happens all the time.) Always leave sufficient time for copious revisions, should they prove necessary. Above all, never be frightened to criticize.

One of the most heinous of delegating sins is being too soft on subordinates. Far too many executives, either because they don't want to hurt their subordinates' feelings or because they don't have the bottle, accept work which they know to be imperfect, and then change it secretly, behind the subordinate's back; or they let it go forward and then blame the subordinate (again probably behind his back) when somebody else tears the proposal apart.

Such spinelessness harms rather than helps the subordinate; it justifiably demolishes the executive's reputation as a manager; and it wastes time. Harvard Professor David McClelland – one of the world's foremost experts in management motivation techniques – published an article called 'Good Guys Make Bum Bosses'[23], and the title says it all.

In contrast, one of the most motivating forms of training delegation, sometimes called 'soft' delegation, is asking subordinates to help you with a knotty problem which has got you temporarily stumped. The request should be made informally, even casually, almost as though you were asking a favour from a friend: 'If you can help me solve this one I'll be eternally grateful – but don't worry about it if you can't. I'll need any ideas you have, though, by next Friday . . .'

Such soft delegation is stimulating, flattering and produces results. A sophisticated development of soft delegation was employed by Robert Magaven when he became head of the superefficient American Safeway food store chain and told his divisional managers: 'I don't know anything about the grocery business but you fellows do. From now on you're running your divisions as if they were your own businesses. You don't take orders from anyone but me and I'm not going to give you orders. I'm going to hold you responsible.' That's reward and punishment and carrot and stick all neatly bundled up in one.

KEY TIP   When delegating, always ask those involved to set their own timetable and then cut it by about 20 per cent (one day in five). As well as speeding things up, a desirable aim in itself, this will stretch people and keep them on their toes without causing undue stress and strain. (And if the ten-day job truly cannot be completed in eight days – a rare occurrence – you can be sure you will be told so vehemently.)

IMPROVEMENT

Helping those who work with and for you to improve their performance will directly help you improve yours. This too derives, you will doubtless by now have recognized, from the crucial contribution of other people to your superefficiency.

In order to help people improve it is essential to think in terms of gardening rather than manufacturing. People are not machines: their minds and motives cannot be restructured and reshaped as if they were physical objects.

'Human engineering' is a fatuous phrase, implying a scientific causality which does not and never will exist. It's all right in science fiction but it won't work in the sales department. (Science fiction is fiction, not science.)

That is why gardening is a far better management analogy. As a gardener you can provide the circumstances which will encourage your plants to maximize their potential, or you can mishandle them and stunt their growth. You do not have the power to turn an onion into a tomato, but you do have the power to grow the best tomatoes in town. As Douglas MacGregor writes in his classic work, *The Human Side of Enterprise*[24]:

> The job environment of the individual is the most important factor affecting his development. Unless that environment is conducive to his growth, none of the other things we do to him or for him will be effective.

Professor Peter Drucker puts much the same point still more succinctly[25]: 'Development is always self-development.'

So you can best help people improve if you help them improve themselves. This has already been stressed in the sections on motivation (*self*-fulfilment and *self*-esteem) and on delegation (*soft* delegation).

The two cardinal concepts involved in helping people (and plants) to maximize their potential are discipline and encouragement. Discipline has already been mentioned several times above: it must be clear, specific, firm, honest and objective. Encouragement is sometimes – particularly during annual appraisals – almost more difficult.

This is because it is so vital (see 'Praise the praiseworthy' – 'But don't overdo it', page 138) to get the tone right. In their efforts to encourage, managers often become ingratiating or pompous, using vague, Victorian schoolmaster clichés. If you can remember seeing the words on your school report, don't use them ('. . . a good effort . . . some worthwhile work . . . steady progress . . . must try harder', and the rest). Such phrases, instead of developing a bond, will emphasize the distance between you and your subordinate and will hinder rather than help achieve persuasive communication. It is vital to be as relaxed, colloquial and unstuffy as you know how, and this is especially true if there is a significant age gap between you.

All of the foregoing are elements of leadership, the fifth principle of management, to which we will now turn.

LEADERSHIP

So many books have been written and so many theories advanced about leadership that it is impossible to do complete justice to the subject here. Having entered this proviso, we must none the less study the principal precepts of leadership, which many psychologists have analysed over recent years but which have not fundamentally changed over hundreds of centuries.

Throughout history thinkers have debated whether leaders are born or made. Indubitably some individuals have the quality called *charisma*. ('Charisma' incidentally, a much misused word, literally means 'a gift from God', in other words, something you are born with, not something that can be acquired.) Charismatic leaders – like Julius Caesar and Joan of Arc, Adolf Hitler and Alexander the Great – are born with some peculiar quality which makes people follow wherever they lead. Whether charisma is a unique quality which differentiates those who have it from those who don't, or whether it is a universal quality which almost everybody has in some degree (like intelligence) but which some people have vastly more of than others, are questions that have never been resolved. (I happen to believe the latter.) In any event, whether you have charisma or not, you can unquestionably be taught to be a better leader, just as quite average army officers can be taught to be highly effective leaders in battle.

To be effective, leaders must initiate and they must have consideration. Here is a thirty-point definition of leader behaviour. The more closely you can follow it, the more effective your leadership will be.

Initiation   Good leaders:

make their attitudes clear to staff
try out new ideas with staff
criticize poor work
assign staff members to particular tasks
speak in a manner not to be questioned
maintain definite standards of performance
emphasize the meeting of deadlines
encourage the use of uniform procedures
ensure their role in the organization is understood by
   all
ask staff to follow standard rules and regulations
let staff members know what is expected of them
ensure staff members are working to full capacity
ensure that work is coordinated
never work without a mental plan
are willing to make necessary changes.

Consideration   Good leaders:

do personal favours for staff members
do little things that make employment more pleasant
are easy to understand
find time to listen
are concerned with the personal welfare of staff
are willing to explain their actions and decisions
are quick to accept new ideas
are friendly and approachable
treat all staff as equals
make staff feel at ease when talking with them
put good suggestions made by staff into operation
seek staff approval on important matters before going
   ahead
are not hermits
can be persuaded of having been wrong
never rule with an iron fist.

These thirty points might be described as a job specification for the perfect leader, and perfect leaders are, like unicorns, mythical beings. But as we've stated in regard to many other aspects of superefficiency, the unattainability of perfection is no excuse for throwing in the towel.

KEY TIP Select the three leadership qualities you know you could most easily improve and give yourself three months to improve them. And after that, how about trying the next three. . .?

The five principles of people management – motivation, organization, delegation, improvement and leadership – have provided guidelines which will greatly enhance your relationships, particularly with colleagues and subordinates. There are, however, in addition two groups of people who demand special consideration: secretaries and bosses.

Secretaries

Most people agree that the three most important people in executives' lives are their spouses, their bosses and their secretaries. Those who disagree generally believe secretaries to be far more important than spouses and bosses.

So the first essential is to select a good one. Some experts would argue that the word 'good' is wrong and the word 'right' would be better: you must select a secretary who is *right* for you, because every boss's needs are different. My experience contradicts this view. Good secretaries are good for everyone, bad secretaries are gruesome.

Obviously it is preferable to find a secretary whose personality you find compatible. However compatibility is far less essential than competence. And excellent secretaries are so scarce that it is idiocy to be too fussy about personality.

The single secretarial skill which outweighs all the

others put together is typing ability: speed, accuracy and layout. If a secretary's typing is slow she will always be behindhand and never have time to do the other things she should be doing; if her typing is inaccurate, endless time will be wasted in retyping everything and inevitably her bloomers won't always be spotted; and if she has no eye for layout her letters (*your* letters) will look insignificant and amateurish.

So before you employ a secretary check her typing yourself. Don't rely on the personnel or secretarial departments. Their standards of layout may not be as high as yours; their accuracy requirements may not be as demanding as yours; they may just want to fill this job so they can get on with the next one – who knows? But it is you who will carry the can when she transforms 'Ready sales in Somerset' into 'Red sails in the sunset'.

If her typing is perfect, the likelihood is that she won't be daft, her shorthand (if any) will be OK and her filing will be sensible, because all those things usually seem to go together. The only remaining significant trait is her telephone manner, and this again is worth checking carefully. Unfortunately it is difficult to check.

KEY TIP If it is feasible, arrange for any prospective secretary to handle your calls for a couple of hours before employing her. If the fates are kind to you (and unkind to her), during that couple of hours you will receive calls from at least one irate customer, one unwanted life insurance salesman, and one muddled employee from another department who is sure you are someone you aren't: a perfect test.

Having selected your secretary, who is as near to perfection as is possible at the ridiculous salary the company is willing to pay, we must assume that she knows the secretarial ropes and can cope competently with day-to-day office routine. (That, after all, is why you chose her.)

In addition to all the important rules and guidelines

mentioned above (especially, once again, 'Praise the praiseworthy, but don't overdo it') here are seven special maxims to help you keep your secretary blissfully happy:

Keep her busy Good secretaries get bored doing nothing, and the devil makes work for ideal hands. (She'll probably start typing out job applications.)

Keep her informed Tell her where you're going, who is coming, what your plans are, why things are happening. She neither can, nor will want to, do her job if you don't.

Don't keep interrupting Give her a pile of work and let her get on with it, then build up another workpile. Don't give it to her in bits and pieces, which is both irritating and inefficient.

Don't waste her time Market research surveys among secretaries always reveal their pet hate to be bosses who waste their time – summoning them for dictation and then rushing into another office, or asking them to stand by for an urgent job and then forgetting to tell them it has been postponed.

Don't start work at 4.30 Good secretaries do not like leaving jobs uncompleted overnight, but neither do they like regularly working late because of their bosses' incompetence. Have a lengthy work session with her immediately the post has been cleared in the morning, and most of the work will be completed that day.

Delegate, delegate Get her to handle as many different jobs on her own initiative as you possibly can (and dare); find non-routine jobs for her, but don't ask her to run messages except when it is absolutely vital, and don't get her involved in private family matters unless and until you know her well.

Trust her This is a corollary of 'Keep her informed', but is much more demanding. Good secretaries learn – if they are not born that way – to be extraordinarily secretive. In business matters you can, should and must trust them unreservedly. If you don't, they will most definitely discover it, and resent it, and either leave or, what is worse, decide the things you are deigning to tell them cannot be terribly secret so they might as well blurt them out.

Finally, if your organization has never arranged a showing of John Cleese's hilarious Video Arts training film *The Secretary and her Boss*, do whatever it takes to organize it. Then watch your secretary laugh uproariously each time Cleese emulates one of your many failings (and restrain yourself from laughing too hilariously at hers).

Bosses

Early in my career one of my clients, who happened to be Japanese, gave me a brief for a new advertising campaign. Partly perhaps because he was Japanese and our communication was far from perfect, I decided to ignore his brief almost entirely and instead devised a campaign I believed to be wonderful. When I presented the campaign to him and his team, the client grew furious, accused me, with justice, of utterly ignoring him, and palpably toyed with the attractive notion of firing me on the spot.

The next day his senior subordinate, who was English, telephoned and inquired why I had attempted to commit hara-kiri. Apart from any other considerations, he said, his boss was livid because I had placed him in an impossible position in front of his subordinates.

I explained, rather primly, that I had merely produced a campaign I believed to be right. Surely that was my job?

'Neither you nor I,' the subordinate replied, 'is likely to get to the top of the tree by trying to face down our bosses and prove them wrong in public.'

Point taken, and learned. It is essential to become adept at handling your boss (in that case a client) if you wish to be successful and superefficient. That is not a recipe for grovelling, toadying servility. It is, on the contrary, a firm recommendation: if you want to get things done your own way, you will usually need to win the agreement of your boss.

(If you consistently fail to win the agreement of your boss, you will consistently fail to get things done your own way. This may be your boss's fault, in which case you may have no alternative but to change jobs; on the other hand, it may not be your boss's fault . . .)

Winning your boss's agreement is much like winning anyone else's agreement. You will need to deploy all the skills of persuasive communication you know. Additionally, however, you must:

Establish how recommendations should be presented Should you communicate verbally or in writing? If in writing, with full documentation or in summary? Does your boss prefer to be kept in touch with ideas as they progress or only to see them when they have been fully developed?

Establish likes and dislikes, quirks and prejudices In other words, you should treat your boss like a customer. If you are going to say something that will irritate, do so knowingly rather than blindly.

Get your timing right Is your boss a lark or an owl? It is rarely advisable to bring bad news at the end of a long, hard day. Check your boss's mood in advance by asking his secretary, and make sure she is on your side. Secretaries can be powerful enemies.

Decide when you need support Some bosses are more easily persuaded by groups putting across a case in concert; others prefer to deal with individuals on a one-to-one basis and are irritated by mobs.

Accept ideas and amendments Very many executives foolishly try to defend their proposals to the death and stubbornly resist every change their boss suggests, whether good, bad or indifferent. Such behaviour betokens desperate insecurity; wise subordinates warmly welcome suggestions that make sense.

Avoid provoking open confrontation   As my opening anecdote showed, it is always dumb to try to put your boss on the spot in front of others. If you feel that you can no longer avoid engaging him in metaphorical fisticuffs, do so privately – and get your timing right (and be sure to have a BATNA ready).

Finally, on the subject of handling bosses, you will obviously win their agreement more easily if you have a good relationship with them, and you are likely to have a good relationship with them if you follow the following six simple rules:

Keep them informed when things are going wrong: never spring disasters on them

Always admit errors: if your boss once suspects you of lying about your mistakes, you will not be trusted again

When your boss has made a mistake, don't rub it in or say, 'I told you so;' there are privileges to being a boss (and that's why you want to become one)

Sometimes deliver jobs before they are needed; if you always go right to the deadline, your boss will notice and is unlikely to be impressed

Be loyal: loyalty may be old-fashioned but it is not out of date, and people who are disloyal to their bosses win nobody's respect. (If you cannot be loyal, leave.)

Turn problems into solutions: never take your boss a problem until you've tried hard to think of a solution; if you cannot think of one, say so, but never never find yourself having a solution suggested that you yourself could easily have thought of if you had bothered.

With your colleagues, subordinates, secretary and boss firmly under control, let us conclude this chapter on people management by forsaking your ambitions and motives and analysing other people's.

Other People's Motives

One of the best bits of advice I have ever received was given to me by one of my earliest bosses, who said, 'While you're listening to what people say, always think of why they are saying it.'

The recommendation to conduct such continuous mental contortions is not as difficult as it may sound. Once again, with practice it comes naturally. It does however involve three dangerous risks:

Paying too little attention to what is said
Ascribing manipulative motives where none exists
Jumping to conclusions.

PAYING TOO LITTLE ATTENTION TO WHAT IS SAID

Many people in organizations become far too fascinated by, and even obsessed with, the politics and power struggles. They forget that the purpose of any organization is to perform efficiently and to achieve its goals; they begin to believe that the manoeuvres and manipulations are ends in themselves. Such individuals – there are many of them in any large organization – often call themselves 'people people', love gossip and tittle-tattle, and are much more interested in who is doing what to whom than in what is being achieved by the organization as a whole. It is as self-destructive to become completely obsessed by internal politics as it is to ignore them completely. Beware.

ASCRIBING MANIPULATIVE MOTIVES WHERE NONE EXISTS

A common by-product of such obsessive behaviour is to perceive plots and politics where none exists. While not at all decrying my early boss's advice, it is vital to remember that many people – perhaps most people – are neither devious nor cunning, and act as they act for the reasons they openly state. (Naturally you can if you wish play amateur psychoanalyst and try to assess their deeper emotions in Freudian or other terms; but we are here considering controllable conscious motives, not uncontrollable subconscious motivations.) When trying to analyse what people are up to, always consider the possibility that they are not up to anything at all.

JUMPING TO CONCLUSIONS

The final and fundamental danger in second-guessing other people's motives is that guessing wrongly will lead you to the wrong conclusions and the wrong decisions – which is why it is often safer and wiser not to second-guess them in the first place. However, on those occasions when it is essential to take at least a cockshy at analysing somebody's motives, the best way to do so is to use a system similar to Benjamin Franklin's decision-maker.

Write down every possible motive for their action or decision, from the most obvious to the most ludicrously unlikely, listing possible positive motives (gains and benefits) on the left, negative motives (avoidance of risks and dangers) on the right. Take some time making the lists. Obviously you must take into account what you know about the person's character and ambitions, likes and dislikes, personal relations with other staff, position in the organizational hierarchy and so on. And remember to include the possibility that the person has simply acted straightforwardly, with no ulterior motive at all.

Once you have completed your lists you will almost always find that some of the items on either side contradict each other and cancel each other out; others won't quite fit with your assessment of the person's personality, or are too foolish or too clever by half; others have implications beyond your control, about which you can do nothing; still others will just seem, on mature reflection, unlikely. Cross all those out.

You will now usually find yourself with two or three

possible motives, any or all of which could be 'correct'. You may be able to whittle this shortlist down to one, which your knowledge and your instincts tell you is the fundamental motive at work. If you can, do so, and act upon your decision. If you cannot, you will have forced yourself to avoid jumping to a rash and dangerous conclusion, and you will be ready for all eventualities.

Psychological studies consistently prove that one person's expectations of another's behaviour strongly affect how that other person behaves. How you treat other people will communicate what you expect of them far more convincingly than anything you say to them.

The secret of handling people superefficiently is to have high expectations of them. They will interpret this to mean that you admire their abilities and respect the way they do things. Not surprisingly, in return they will willingly work like hell for you and you will all win. That's superefficient people management.

SUPEREFFICIENCY
CAN BE YOURS

Earlier on a brief reference was made to a study of how executives spend their time, published in 1979 in the *IBM Systems Journal*[20]. You will see the complete analysis on the opposite page.

All the asterisked activities have been covered in *Superefficiency* and (excluding 'other') they account for 92.5 per cent of top management's time and 78.6 per cent of all executives' time. In other words, far and away the bulk of your working week.

So if *Superefficiency* improves your efficiency by 10 per cent, a modest enough target, you will increase your productivity by 8-9 per cent – that's an extra month gained each year.

Naturally you won't suddenly encounter a yawning chasm every eleven months. You will simply find yourself with extra time to plan and be creative, extra time to delegate and handle people considerately, extra time to think, to manage and to relax, unencumbered by continual crises, confusion, catastrophes and chaos.

Activities	Time spent on activities	
	Top management (%)	All executives (%)
Writing*	9.8	15.6
Mail handling*	6.1	4.4
Proofreading	1.8	2.3
Searching	3.0	5.6
Reading*	8.7	7.3
Filing*	1.1	2.0
Retrieving filed information*	1.8	3.6
Dictating to secretary*	4.9	1.9
Dictating to a machine*	1.0	0.6
Telephone*	13.8	12.3
Calculating	2.3	6.6
Conferring with secretary*	2.9	1.8
Scheduled meetings*	13.1	7.0
Unscheduled meetings*	8.5	5.4
Planning or scheduling*	4.7	4.3
Travelling*	13.1	6.4
Copying	0.1	0.9
Using equipment	0.1	4.4
Other	3.2	7.6
	100.0	100.0

It is now possible to define the seven techniques with which you can turn the seven keys, and identifying them will be helpful as a means to recapitulate the principal messages of the book. They are, in alphabetical order:

Analysis
Development
Listings
Preparation
Prioritization
Self-discipline
Willpower.

Analysis This is essential to decision-making, problem-solving and idea development; to communication (think out what you wish to communicate before you write and speak); to time management; and to the study of other people's motives.

Development You should develop those talents and skills you can easily improve: personal communication, writing, presentations, speech-making and salesmanship; maximizing creativity and managing people.

Listings Using lists takes the strain off your memory, helps you to break down problems and build up ideas, and above all guides your schedule of activities from day to day.

Preparation You should be ready for unpleasant tasks and BATNAs; for negotiation, dictation and computerization; for commuting and international travel; for effective filing; for meetings. 'Preparation' is a synonym for that all-important word: 'rehearsal'.

Prioritization One of the fundamentals of superefficiency is the ever present problem of deciding what to do in what order – coping with interruptions, how to deal with the paper jungle, what to read, which jobs to deal with and which to dump.

Self-discipline This is the prerequisite for overcoming laziness and defeating procrastination, for keeping a tight rein on telephone chatter and office gossip, for helping you to fight absent-mindedness and to find extra time in the day; and for developing the vital qualities of leadership, organization and motivation.

Willpower Another concept, like 'loyalty', which is old-fashioned but not out of date, willpower is the mainspring of superefficiency, the crucial foundation upon which all self-improvement is built.

With these far from superhuman techniques you can deftly turn the seven keys – persuasive communication, time management, defeating procrastination, mastering data, having winning ideas, creative travelling and handling people – that will open all the locks which used to bar your way to superefficiency.

Superefficiency is not, however, a mechanical process. Human beings, as we have noted before, are not robots; perfection is unattainable.

Superefficiency *is* attainable. And with superefficiency you will be able to manage yourself, to maximize your abilities, your potential and your success. From now on your working life will be less shambolic, less frustrating, better organized – and much, much more fun.

NOTES

1 M. Argyle, V. Satter, H. Nicholson, M. Williams and P. Burgess, 'The Communication of Inferior and Superior Attitudes by Verbal and Non-verbal Signals', *British Journal of Social and Clinical Psychology*, pages 222-231, 1970.
2 Robert C. Beck, *Applying Psychology: Understanding People*, Prentice-Hall, New Jersey, 1982.
3 Study by Westinghouse Electric Corporation, in Roy V. Hughson, *Effective Communications for Engineers*, McGraw-Hill, New York, 1974.
4 A.A. Harrison, *Individuals and Groups*, Brooks/Cole, California, 1976.
5 Peter F. Drucker, *The Effective Executive*, William Heinemann, London, 1967.
6 W.J. McGuire, 'The Nature of Attitudes and Attitude Change', in *Handbook of Social Psychology* (ed. G. Lindzey and E. Aronson), Addison-Wesley, Massachusetts, 1969.
7 Harry Turner, *The Gentle Art of Salesmanship*, Fontana, London, 1985.
8 Professor H.A. Overstreet, *Influencing Human Behaviour*, W.W. Norton & Co., New York.
9 Peter Turla and Kathleen L. Hawkins, *Time Management Made Easy*, Panther Books, London, 1985.
10 Lee Iacocca, *Iacocca, An Autobiography*, Sidgwick & Jackson, London, 1985.

11 Kenneth Blanchard and Spencer Johnson, *The One Minute Manager*, Fontana, London, 1983.
12 Karen O'Quin and Joel Aronoff, in *Social Psychology Quarterly*, USA, vol. 44, no. 4, 1981.
13 Roger Fisher and William Ury, *Getting to Yes: Negotiating Agreement Without Giving In*, Hutchinson & Co., London, 1982.
14 Robert Ornstein, *Psychology of Consciousness*, W.H. Freeman & Co., Oxford, 1972.
15 Arthur Koestler, *The Act of Creation*, Hutchinson & Co., London, 1964.
16 Edward de Bono, *Lateral Thinking for Management*, Penguin Books, London, 1982.
17 J. Geoffrey Rawlinson, *Creative Thinking and Brainstorming*, John Wiley & Sons, New York, 1981.
18 Alex F. Osborn, *Applied Imagination*, Charles Scribner's Sons, New York, 1957.
19 Sidney J. Parnes, *Creative Behaviour Guidebook*, Charles Scribner's Sons, New York, 1967.
20 G. Engel, J. Groppuso, R. Lowenstein and W. Traub, 'An Office Communications System', in *IBM Systems Journal*, vol. 18, no. 3, 1979.
21 Abraham H. Maslow, *A Theory of Human Motivation*, Penguin Books, London, 1970.
22 Robert Townsend, *Up the Organization*, Michael Joseph, London, 1971.
23 David McClelland, 'Good Guys Make Bum Bosses', in *Selected Papers: Motives, Personality and Society*, Praeger, New York, 1984.
24 Douglas MacGregor, *The Human Side of Enterprise*, McGraw-Hill, New York, 1960.
25 Peter F. Drucker, *The Practice of Management*, William Heinemann, London, 1955.